MARCO POLO

METROPOLIS

Travel with
**Insider
Tips**

MADRID

ATLANTIC
OCEAN

FRANCE

Bilbao

PORTUGAL

ANDORRA

Lisbon

Madrid

Barcelona

SPAIN

Valencia

Balearic I.
(E)

Málaga

MOROCCO *Mediterranean
Sea*

I0412324

www.marco-polo.com

SYMBOLS

 INSIDER TIP Insider Tip

★ Highlight

⚫⚫⚫⚫ Best of...

☼ Scenic view

♲ Responsible travel: for ecological or fair trade aspects

(*) Telephone numbers that are not toll-free

PRICE CATEGORIES HOTELS

Expensive	over 130 euros
Moderate	80–130 euros
Budget	under 80 euros

The prices are for a double room per night without breakfast

PRICE CATEGORIES RESTAURANTS

Expensive	over 40 euros
Moderate	20–40 euros
Budget	under 20 euros

Prices for a three course meal without drinks

On the cover: Spectacular "floating" Cultural Centre p. 29 | Trendy Triball p. 42

CONTENTS

MAPS IN THE GUIDEBOOK
(122 A1) Page numbers and coordinates refer to the street atlas and the map of Madrid and the surrounding area on p. 134/135
(0) Site/address located off the map
Coordinates are also given for places that are not marked on the street atlas

(*(□ A–B 2–3)*) refers to the removable pull-out map

INSIDE FRONT COVER:
The best Highlights

INSIDE BACK COVER:
Metro map

The best MARCO POLO Insider Tips

Our top 15 Insider Tips

INSIDER TIP **Singing waiters**

Opera arias on the menu: professional singers serve you your dinner in the atmospheric *La Favorita* restaurant → **p. 59**

INSIDER TIP **Visit an enchanted garden**

Discover the *El Capricho de la Alameda de Osuna* – a park with romantic ruins, fountains and a labyrinth – tucked away between the trade fair grounds and the airport → **p. 51**

INSIDER TIP **Watch an Egyptian sunset**

Come to the far side of the city forest Casa de Campo and watch the setting sun bathing the *Templo de Debod* in its golden light – there is no better place to be (photo above) → **p. 45**

INSIDER TIP **Fairytale beds**

21st century comfort housed in 19th century architecture: The *Posada del Dragón* is one of Madrid's most stylish hotels → **p. 86**

INSIDER TIP **Sweets with God's blessing**

Delicious biscuits and pastries, jams and other sweet delicacies are still produced in many of Spain's monasteries. Slightly off the beaten track in the old town is the tiny shop *El Jardín del Convento* which sells handmade delicacies in pretty, old-fashioned packaging → **p. 69**

INSIDER TIP **Manifestation in surrealism**

The Museo Reina Sofía (photo right) exhibits contemporary art including the 16-minute film *Un chien Andalou* created by Salvador Dalí and Luis Buñuel which is just as fascinating today as it was in 1929 on its release → **p. 48**

INSIDER TIP **City panorama**

The *Gourmet Experience Gran Vía* serves delicious food accompanied by a spectacular view on the 9th floor of the El Corte Inglés department store → **p. 61**

INSIDER TIP **The best of the barrios**

Malasaña is not a rich area but a trendy district among Madrid's young locals who head down the *Calle Espíritu Santo* looking for something out-of-the-ordinary → p. 68

INSIDER TIP **Strong smells**

The *Quesería Conde Duque* is a treat for the eyes, nose and taste buds: cheese from all over Spain is sold here, fresh and lovingly prepared → p. 69

INSIDER TIP **Sensual fabrics**

Fashion designer Paloma del Pozo creates extravagance to wear: buy it in the small boutique in Huertas, the *Ojalá* → p. 72

INSIDER TIP **Hidden art**

Madrid is one of the world's art capitals. Besides its famous art galleries, the city is home to other smaller museums, often overlooked by locals, such as the *Museo Lázaro Galdiano,* which would be a sensation in any other city → p. 50

INSIDER TIP **Coffee and cinema**

The *Ocho y Medio* (named after Federico Fellini's film 8 ½) located on Madrid's "Walk of Fame" is where the city's movie buffs meet up with a book shop specialising in film literature and a cosy coffee shop → p. 81

INSIDER TIP **Flamenco in the park**

The biggest flamenco artists perform at the Veranos de la Villa in the *Jardines de Sabatini* next to the Royal Palace in July and August → p. 107

INSIDER TIP **Final place of rest**

The *Cementerio de San Isidro* is a historic cemetery with pompous, partly crumbling gravestones and interspersed with fantastic views over the city → p. 97

INSIDER TIP **Relaxing steps**

In a pretty corner of the Barrio de los Austrias, you will find the *Café del Nuncio* where the tables outside invite you to take a break → p. 57

BEST OF...

FOR FREE

● *Contemporary and experimental arts*
Once a slaughterhouse, the *Matadero Madrid* has been successfully transformed into a platform for artists, performers, designers and other creative minds to flesh out their ideas. Visitors can also enjoy the exhibitions and events held there → p. 81

● *Art in the park*
Reina Sofía is one of the world's best museums for 20th and 21st century art. The most important works are in the main building on the edge of Lavapiés but the museum also has two branches in Retiro, the *Palacio de Velázquez* and the *Palacio de Cristal,* where special exhibitions are often showing and admission is free → p. 36

● *Live like kings*
Madrid would not be Madrid without its kings. Philip II of Spain turned the small town into Spain's capital in 1561. 200 years later Philip V commissioned the modern *Palacio Real* which today is virtually in the hands of tourists. From Monday to Thursday, EU citizens can visit the palace for free in the last two hours before closure → p. 38

● *A peek into the Prado*
Before heading out to your nightly *marcha* why not stop by the *Museo del Prado* to admire some of the famous pictures that you've always wanted to see in real life. It won't put a dent in your pocket – entry 2is free between 6pm (Sundays from 5pm) and 8pm! (photo) → p. 32

● *Back in time to the 19th century*
Stroll through the *Museo Cerralbo* and experience the enviable lifestyle of a 19th century marquis – admission is free on Sundays and on Saturdays between 2pm and 3pm → p. 44

● *Public living room*
The sofas, armchairs and lounge zones in the new *Centro Centro* at the Plaza de Cibeles are extremely popular with locals mainly due to the daily newspapers and free WiFi available → p. 33

● *Chocolate con churros*

What better way to round off a night on the town than with *chocolate con churros*? The *Chocolatería San Ginés* between the Puerta del Sol and Plaza Mayor is one of the city's most popular places. The thick creamy potion served here is not hot chocolate but is actually for dunking the *churros* – a longish, delicious, deep-fried pastry. Heavenly! → p. 76

● *As in Goya's day*

The *Fiesta de San Isidro* is an occasion for the residents of Madrid to don their traditional outfits. The fiesta is held in May and honours the city's patron, locals make a picnic pilgrimage to the Ermita de San Isidro across the river Manzanares in a scene reminiscent of Goya's "La Pradera de San Isidro" gracing the Prado → p. 106

● *Live like there is no tomorrow*

Seeing is believing: there are traffic jams on the Gran Vía in the middle of the night; the alleyways and streets of Madrid's *centro* are jam-packed with late night revellers and it is not only the young. Drop in at one of the many open air *terrazas* like the *Atenas* and you will see Madrileños of all ages up until the early hours of the morning → p. 77

● *Meeting place for intellectuals*

There is no trace of the small tobacco kiosk that once marked the entrance to the *Café Gijón*. But even without the smoke, this iconic coffee shop remains one of Madrid's intellectual institutions. Made famous over the past 130 years by the likes of Camilo José Cela and Ortega y Gasset → p. 58

● *A second-hand world*

Madrid's main flea market, the *Rastro,* is an institution, a ritual that goes far beyond the mundane of buying and selling. You will find whatever your heart desires – you need only look long enough (photo) → p. 69

● *Tapas tasting*

Eating out and going out become one thing when you do as the locals do and go on a *tapeo* – a tour of all the various tapas bars – a mandatory stop has to be the *Cava Baja* in the La Latina district → p. 65

ONLY IN

BEST OF...

● Marvels of modern art

The *Museo Nacional Centro de Arte Reina Sofía* is not only the place where you can view famous works by the two masters Dalí and Picasso – and of course his "Guernica" – the gallery hosts a dizzying array of contemporary art, focusing on the movement's themes, utopias and tyrannies → **p. 47**

● A famed soccer club

If you have ever wanted to see where Cristiano Ronaldo trains then you are in for a treat with the guided tour of Real Madrid's *Bernabéu stadium* → **p. 24**

● Coming to the big screen

The *Capitol* in the Gran Vía is Madrid's most famous cinema where all the premieres are held. Its main theatre with a gallery recalls the glitz and glamour of Hollywood's heyday in the 1950s → **p. 80**

● Café society

The *Círculo de Bellas Artes* owns what has to be the most beautiful café in the city. Beneath painted ceilings and crystal chandeliers it hardly matters that the waiters here really take their time. At some point you can then take in the exhibitions and cultural programmes (photo) → **p. 81**

● Tropical garden

Even if it rains, you will stay dry and warm – the *Estación de Atocha* is now the departure point for the high-speed Ave train to Seville and this old station has come into its own as a lush, green conservatory → **p. 46**

● Shopping centre

Fashion, furniture, cosmetics, gastronomy and cinema all under one roof: one hour will soon turn into three in *Príncipe Pío,* the city centre's largest shopping centre at the train station with the same name → **p. 70**

RAIN

● *Royal gardens*
Nothing against Retiro – but sometimes it feels like you're at a funfair. If you're in search of peace, head to the *Campo del Moro* gardens beneath the Palacio Real → **p. 37**

● *Bathe as the Moors once did*
Take a trip back to the Madrid of the Moors and visit the Arabian baths *Hammam Al Andalus*. Relax in hot water baths beneath ancient stone arches and forget the noise of the city for one and a half hours. Then treat yourself to a heavenly massage → **p. 79**

● *Lazy day on the lake*
The *Estanque* is really just a large pond so rowing in the Retiro park can never be mistaken as a sport but instead a form of urban meditation: dip your oar in the water a few times and then let go and allow yourself to drift off → **p. 104**

● *Cool off*
Don't let the heat get to you. If your hotel or guest house lacks a swimming pool simply make your way to the Casa de Campo for a dip in the city's most inviting *public swimming pool* → **p. 35**

● *Open-top tour*
This is the perfect way to get a first impression of Madrid whilst resting your weary feet! Sit back and relax and let the open-top double decker bus of the *Madrid City Tour* take you an entire round through the city's historic centre → **p. 112**

● *Cable car*
The *Teleférico* cable car has connected the Parque del Oeste and the Casa de Campo since 1969, taking passengers over the treetops to the heart of Madrid's city forest and offering splendid views of the Royal Palace and the Sierra de Guadarrama mountain range → **p. 105**

INTRUDUCTION

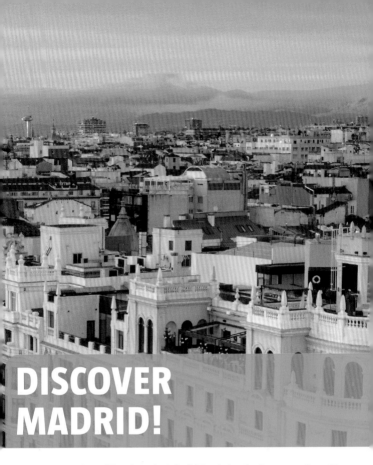

DISCOVER MADRID!

If you happen to be walking along the Calle del Pez during the day, you are bound to come across Ramón. Ramón leads a busy life but he always makes the time to compliment those passing by. "How beautiful you look today Señora!" is his catch phrase to the ladies – young and old but especially to the older women. You'll see him peeping into prams and asking the mothers, "How is the little one today?" As for the men dashing off to the office, he'll spur them on with, "It's off to work we go!" Nobody considers Ramón a nuisance and everyone happily responds to his greetings with an amused smile. The shopkeepers also play their part by giving him the odd errand to run: deliver a loaf of bread, take waste paper to the recycler or distribute a free newspaper. Ramón is simply regarded as an integral part of the Calle del Pez.

Do not believe a word the Madrileños say about their city. "The city is falling to pieces!" they claim and complain about the dirt, the bad state of the roads and the city's politicians. One particularly unpopular one is Ana Botella, the former mayor of Madrid who gave a very embarrassing speech about Madrid to representatives of the International Olympic Committee in 2013. She claimed "Madrid is fun!" and invited visitors to enjoy a "relaxing cup of *café con leche* in Plaza Mayor" – the video went viral and caught her pulling a face like she was on much stronger drugs than just a cup of white coffee. In the end the 2020 Summer Olympics went to Tokyo.

In reality the Madrileños are extremely proud of their city as in fact are all Spaniards of their hometowns. That said, the Spanish capital has indeed seen better days yet

> **Crisis? Madrid has held onto its joie de vivre**

that's not Ana Botella's fault. She took over the office of city mayor from her extremely popular predecessor, Alberto Ruiz-Gallardón, in 2011 when Madrid, and in fact the whole country, was in a deep crisis. Ruiz-Gallardón had a natural instinct for what the residents of Madrid wanted for their city. He had the ambitious plan to move sections of the ring motorway, which had run along the banks of the Manzanares River for decades, into an underground tunnel. The reclaimed ground above the tunnel was transformed into a *park at the foot of the old town*, giving Madrid a revamped and more attractive city landscape.

On the downside the project costs spiralled, leaving the city with debts of over 7 billion euros. This only confirmed the common perception held by Northern European countries that the South has for a long time been living above its means. Although a somewhat simplified version of affairs, Spain is having to enforce austerity measures.

Life has certainly become harder in Spain yet tourists will not notice a change. *The cafés are full*, the shops are full and the streets are full. The houses and its people all look in good shape. You are sometimes left wondering, where is the crisis? Well for one thing the Metro runs less frequently than it used to and the escalators are constantly not in use. The road surfaces are also in a poor condition yet this is nothing new.

The residents of Madrid will always find something to moan about. They are never satisfied – a trait that can be attributed to most capital-city dwellers in good times as well as bad. Javier Marías, the novelist and Madrid's most famous critic, once wrote that although the city was one big construction site, it was hard to see any improvements. He was proved to be wrong; the manic city development project between the 1990s and early 2000s has paid off, creating a *more enjoyable, pedestrian-friendly and colourful*

place to live. Facades which were once grey now radiate colour and the dark old city streets have been transformed into green spaces. The city's boom has also attracted immigrants mainly from Latin America, Romania, China and Morocco. Although there is some way to go before Madrid can claim to be a cosmopolitan metropolis, it has shaken off some of its provincial feel. Despite many of the immigrants returning to their countries of origin when the crisis hit in 2008 due to the lack of jobs in the city and Spain as a whole, Madrid continues to steer the country's economy.

> **The city became more pedestrian-friendly, more colourful**

Is everything then really so bad? Probably. Madrid's vibrant inner city is just one side. Take a *closer look* and you will see people scavenging for food in dustbins or standing in food kitchen queues. You will not be confronted with poverty and hardship wherever you go, but it still exists: behind the well-kept facades you will find a family of four sharing a one-bedroom apartment or a 50-year old IT specialist who has been unemployed for five years, still living with his mother in his old bedroom. People are surviving but only thanks to families holding together. *Madrid is coping with the crisis* because the poorest have learnt to survive on a shoestring. "Madrid is fun?" Unfortunately not for them.

The equestrian statue of Philip IV looms large in the Plaza de Oriente in front of the Royal Palace

With a population of 3.2 million Madrid is Spain's largest city but its intrinsically *rural roots* still prevail. There are very few families who have lived in the city for generations, most of its citizens have moved there from the countryside and are new arrivals, or the children or grandchildren of new arrivals. It is for this reason that whenever there is a long weekend there is a mass exodus of cars from the city heading out to all the corners of Spain. It is the time when everyone heads *voy al pueblo* – back to the village. Be it the village of their parents, uncles and aunts or grandparents, every Madrid resident has a home town somewhere in Spain.

Ever since Hapsburg King Felipe II chose Madrid – an insignificant small Castilian town – as the capital for his empire in 1561 it has remained a city of immigrants. Over the centuries the *royal court* was perceived as a potential place of work that lured people to the city. However, the living conditions of most of the inhabitants were so miserable that there were more deaths than births. Madrid would never have survived were it not for the constant stream of new arrivals from Galicia,

> **Madrid has a vibrant street life**

Andalusia, Extremadura, the Basque country and the Castilian hinterland. Even so, the city grew very slowly. In 1910 London had a population of more than seven million, Berlin two million but Madrid a mere 500,000.

It would be decades before it would be on a par with other European cities. Spain and Madrid endured both a dramatic civil war from 1936 to 1939 and the subsequent dictatorship of General Francisco Franco. Politically the country was at its lowest ebb and it was only from the 1960s onwards that it was gradually able to show some signs of economic development. After the death of the dictator in 1975, Spain freed itself from 40 years of repression. Madrid experienced an explosion of *a lust for life.* "It was a rash, playful, creative period full of feverish nights," according to cult film director Pedro Almodóvar. For a few years Madrid was the hippest city in the world. Those now in their fifties or sixties still mourn the days of Madrid's counter culture movement, the *Movida Madrileña.* But not only has the *marcha* – long nights of fun and dancing – survived but also a more open mind and spirit. *Chueca, the gay neighbourhood,* is the pride of the city and plays host to Madrid's largest festival, the *Día del Orgullo Gay,* "day of gay pride".

To visitors from the rest of Spain, Madrid seems especially large and loud. Its size is really a question of perspective and the noise is measurable. The Madrid traffic is more annoying than in other cities because it is very built up and its narrow city centre streets have not been able to cope with the city it has become. The traffic also impacts on the poor quality of the air. None of this bothers the locals who drink their coffee on pavement cafés on the Gran Vía or the *terrazas* of the Paseo de Recoletos unperturbed. While the pedestrian zones in other cities are deserted in the evenings and on Sundays, the Spanish capital stays in full swing – the city's inhabitants love being outdoors and their vibrant street life is an institution in itself.

Madrid is, by the way, the highest capital city in Europe (if you exclude San Marino and Andorra la Vella), a plaque on the seat of the regional government at Puerta del Sol reads 650.7 m/2134.8 ft above sea level. Still, its citizens see no reason to regard their city as something special. Moaning is what they like doing best and their favourite past time. So in 2014 when the city administration launched a *public electric bike hire scheme*, it almost

Art, kitsch and bric-a-brac: Rastro belongs to the Sunday morning ritual

caused a revolution: cyclists had been a rare sight in the Spanish capital and were often seen to be risking their lives. The scheme also encountered numerous teething problems at the start: overloaded servers, card readers that couldn't scan cards and clueless customers standing in front of bike-hire stations. The moaners couldn't resist the opportunity, insisting again that nothing works in the city!

> **Madrid is all about *marcha* – dancing the night away**

The scheme's teething troubles were soon ironed out and the city was suddenly awash with bikers, giving the city a livelier and more vibrant feel, in the face of all adversity. *Madrid has refused to give in and has made the most out of this difficult crisis*. The city has held onto its lust for life, a spirit left slightly bruised by the events but one that stands tall in the face of adversity! We will not let the crisis take our pleasures away as well! And so in this respect, Madrid and its inhabitants are gradually finding their tentative way out of the crisis, still slightly under shock yet with the firm conviction that things will improve.

WHAT'S HOT

1 Ginebra

Juniper berry concoctions The Spanish were never particular fussy when it came to Gin. This was until a group of distilleries from Catalonia (Gin Mare), Galicia (Nordés) and even from the home of sherry, Jerez (The London No. 1), was bold enough to try new flavours, experiment with natural aromas and also perfect their label designs. Their efforts have been rewarded in Madrid. The range of gins now available is overwhelming; groups of friends now spend their evenings gin-tasting to keep up with the new trends *(cata de ginebras)*. First point of call: the *Casa del Pez (C/Jesús del Valle 1)* in Malasaña.

Moda de Madrid 2

Extravagant Creative with plenty of attention to detail best defines the designs of Inés and Iván for the label *La Casita de Wendy (www.lacasitadewendy.com / photo)*. Icelandic pop star Björk is a great fan and has even worn some of their creations for the covers of magazines. *García Madrid (www.garciamadrid.com)* specialises in men's fashions. The designer uses his showroom to display his latest creations and art exhibitions as well.

3 Latino rhythms

Bridge over the Atlantic Whenever Latin American music is exported to Europe, the first port of call is always Madrid. Shakira, Juanes or Compay Segundo all became stars in Spain before venturing north of the Pyrenees. The latest import, this time from the Dominican Republic, is a new dance craze, the Salsa-inspired Bachata, which can be heard and seen performed in the small, vibrant dance club *Azúcar (Paseo Reina Cristina 7)*.

De Madrid al cielo

Up on the roof Luis Quiñones de Benavente (1581–1651), the dramatist of the *siglo de oro* – the golden age of Spanish art and literature –, once wrote the verse "From Madrid to the heavens": in other words who needs to see anything else once they have seen Madrid? The fact is Madrid's residents love their city's skyline, preferably seen from one of the city's many roof terraces which never go out of fashion and are constantly reinvented in style. A classic among the classics is the *Círculo de Bellas Artes (C/ de Alcalá 42 | photo)* while the hotel terraces at *ME Reina Victoria (Plaza de Santa Ana 14)* and *Hotel de las Letras (Gran Vía 11)* are for those looking to join an elegant, if not slightly elite crowd. The *Hotel Emperador* offers a roof-top swimming pool *(Mon–Fri 33 euros, Sat/Sun 44 euros | Gran Via 53)*. A combination of chic, retro and slightly tasteless is the terraza on the roof-top of an old cinema in Malasaña: the *Gymage Lounge Resort (C/ de la Luna 2)* is one of the coolest bars in Madrid and guests are oblivious to the fitness fanatics working out one floor below.

4

Molecular

Taste explosion Spain was never known for its experimental cuisine. This was until Ferran Adrià hit the scene. He invented molecular gastronomy, redefined Spanish cuisine and became the world's most famous chef. One of his former employees, Paco Roncero, who has almost achieved the same fame as his master, runs the *La Terraza del Casino (www.casinodemadrid.es)* and *Estado Puro (www.tapasenestadopuro.com | photo)*, which for some is reason in itself to visit Madrid.

5

IN A NUTSHELL

A LMODÓVAR

Pedro Almodóvar is Spain's big name in film making; he was born in 1951 and hails from the countryside but has made the city of Madrid his home. He grew up in a village in La Mancha in the heart of Spain, and he left the countryside at the age of 18, together with his brother, for a new life in the capital. Later Madrid would become the canvas and the subject for many of his films. Homosexuals, transvestites and strong female figures are common protagonists in the films he directs. *Mujeres al borde de un ataque de nervios* ("Women on the Verge of a Nervous Breakdown", 1988) made him famous. His Oscar successes with *Todo sobre mi madre* – "All about my Mother", 1999 – and *Hable con ella* –

"Talk to Her", 2002 – turned him into the star of Spain's cultural scene. Almodóvar is not the provocateur that many see him as; he simply shows life as it is and does it in a very natural style and with great wit.

B ICIMAD

In summer 2014 the El País journalist Pablo León wrote "It's time Madrid gets on its bike." A daring statement in view of the fact that in Europe Madrid had the reputation of being a cyclist's nightmare. Those who valued their life opted to go on foot or by metro. Since then not everything has changed, but many things have. This summer the city administration set up electric hire bike stations all over the city (see p. 110) and

Madrid from A to T – background stories about flamenco and bullfighting, the king and a film-crazy director

believe it or not they were a resounding success. Ever so gradually the Madrileños drivers are becoming accustomed to sharing the road with cyclists. There are however only a handful of cycling lanes, except for the ⊕ *Anillo Verde,* the "green belt", a 64 km/40 miles cycling route around the city. *www.anillo verdeciclista.es*

B OINA
The sun shines the majority of time in Madrid. Yet if you approach the city from one of its suburbs, instead of blue skies, you'll notice a brown smog cloud sitting on top of the city, prompting residents to call this *boina,* or "beret". Although the Spanish capital has been fighting against this smog for decades, progress is painfully slow. Local politicians have continuously shied away from radical measures such as driving bans. This form of action would in fact be necessary to combat the major problem of nitrogen oxygen pollution caused by car exhaust fumes.

CLIMATE

Nueve meses de invierno, tres meses de infierno! It is a fallacy that winter in Madrid is nine months long and that the summer months are infernally hot. But is quite normal in July and August for there to be a few heat waves when it gets up to 40°C/104°F in the shade and the winter months are not Mediterranean mild. They can have a rather rough Castilian nip to them although it would be true to say that the clouds are never as low and heavy in Madrid as they are in Northern Europe.

DOCE UVAS

It is traditional to eat twelve grapes on New Year's Eve, one on each chime as midnight heralds in the *Nochevieja*. The whole of Spain does so simultaneously (as they watch TV) counting down with the Casa de Correos clock on the Puerta del Sol. Entrepreneurs now sell cans with a dozen peeled, seedless grapes just to make the transition into the New Year that much easier. The custom is supposed to bring prosperity to the year ahead and originated in Madrid in the late the 19th century.

FLAMENCO

Vente pa' Madrid (come to Madrid!) are the lyrics of one of the songs of flamenco-pop group Ketama and Madrid has indeed become the unofficial capital of Spain's flamenco artists, although many of them hail from Andalusia where flamenco originated in the second half of the 18th century. It is also where it evolved – between 1860 and 1910 – into today's classical versions. Madrid is where the singers, musicians and dancers find the most important recording studios and the right venues that will give lead to countrywide recognition. Flamenco has opened up to other musical styles and flamenco fusion is one of the most exciting genres of the European music scene. Get a feel for it with Bebo & Cigala's *Lágrimas Negras* (flamenco jazz), Chambao's *Endorfinas en la Mente* (flamenco chill out) and Enrique Morente's *Omega* (flamenco rock). Estrella Morente

Noise and air pollution: the constant stream of traffic on the Calle de Alcalá

sings traditional flamenco with her mellow voice in *Mi Cante y un Poema*. Also a classic: Miguel Poveda, *Sonetos y poemas para la libertad*. In 2014 Paco de Lucía died, the greatest flamenco guitarist of all time. His posthumous album: *Canción Andaluza*. www.deflamenco.com

IMMIGRATION

Even in the mid 1990s anyone sitting in the Madrid Metro would only see Spanish faces around them. It was a provincial city as yet untouched by the flow of people around the world. However this would change dramatically within a couple of years and nowadays Madrid is fast on the road to becoming a cosmopolitan world metropolis. Between 2000 and 2010 the number of foreigners increased from 166,000 to a good 1.1 million. During the economic crisis, Spains attraction as an immigration country has faded somewhat. By now, some 900,000 foreigners live in the Comunidad de Madrid, 13.7 per cent. Less than a quarter of the immigrants are from Romania, followed by new arrivals from Morocco, Ecuador and China. The locals and new arrivals seem to live a tolerant co-existence.

MONARCHY

When the Spanish king Juan Carlos abdicated on 2 June 2014, 20,000 people gathered together in the evening on Madrid's Puerta del Sol to transform the square into a sea of red, yellow and violet flags – the colours of the Second Republic (1931–1939). They were demanding a referendum to decide on the future of the Spanish monarchy. "Juan Carlos has his merits", commented one demonstrator, "but I don't understand why Felipe should automatically become his successor without any questions asked. This is not what I call true democ-

racy." Felipe did however automatically take the throne to become the new Spanish king and most Spaniards are satisfied with the job he has done so far. The fact is that although his father Juan Carlos earned his merits in protecting the Spanish democracy at the end of the Franco dictatorship in 1975, the former king then chose to rest on his laurels. The Spaniards also criticised him for allowing his son-in-law Iñaki Urdangarin to embezzle public funds and faced even more criticism for making an elephant-hunting trip in the middle of the economic crisis. His abdication was an attempt to save the Spanish monarchy. This appears to have paid off: Felipe VI, who is married to the journalist Letizia Ortiz with whom he has two delightful daughters, Leonor and Sofía, is a popular successor because he masters the art of avoiding making mistakes.

NOISE

In Madrid you definitely have it made if you are a sound sleeper. The early morning hours can be a flurry of noisy activity – rubbish removal trucks and cheerful night owls compete to wake residents from their slumber. During the day the city noise reverberates off the buildings – roaring scooters, droning commuter buses and hooting taxis are the order of the day. The only weapon the residents have in their fight against the noise is to keep calm and have a bucket (or a glass at least) of water ready to throw on anyone disturbing the peace.

OSO Y MADROÑO

Madrid's official coat of arms depicts a bear and a strawberry tree and Spanish tourists make a point of being photographed in front of the large life-sized bronze statue on the Puerta del Sol. For the locals the statue, which has only been around since 1967, serves as the perfect meeting point where they are not likely to miss one another.

1 5-M

The abbreviation (spoken *quince eme)* stands for a date: 15 May 2011. On this date ten thousand demonstrators protested through the streets of Madrid demanding *Democracia real YA:* "Real Democracy NOW". A few days later the protestors set up a temporary camp on the Puerta del Sol, signalling the start of the international occupy movement. The protest was aimed at a political system that, according to the demonstrators, had neglected to react to the difficult economic crisis which had taken hold of Spain since 2008. The camp disappeared after two months and the 15-M movement seemed to have collapsed. Yet the movement has remained actively engaged with neighbourhood groups organising protests against house evictions, against the privatisation of the health system or cuts to the education system. The 15-M movement has 'politicised' many Spaniards who had previously shown little interest in politics. When the Madrid-born political scientist Pablo Iglesias founded the *Podemos* party (translated in English as "We can") with other like-minded individuals in January 2014, he already had the support of the network of activists who had united in the aftermath of the 15-M movement – one of the reasons why the Podemos party has emerged from nothing to become one of Spain's most influential political forces. *archivosol15m.wordpress.com*

S IESTA

Ignacio Buqueras has been lobbying to abolish the siesta for many years. The president of Fundación Independiente, a research organization in Madrid that has led the campaign for shorter workdays

LOS GALÁCTICOS

What a club! They have won the Spanish La Liga 32 times, the Spanish trophy 19 times and the Champion's League 10 times. The best club of the 20th century, the Fifa said. Founded in 1902, it now has 92,000 members and has called itself *real* or "royal" since 1920. The Real Madrid stadium was inaugurated in 1947 and can seat 81,000 spectators. It is named after Santiago Bernabéu, the president with the longest (1943–1978) term in office. The easiest way to get tickets for a game is via the Internet *(www.realmadrid.com)* or directly at the stadium. Non-members don't stand a chance when it comes to top matches – except on the black market where tickets sell for up to 500 euros. If you go away empty handed there are always the ● guided tours through the stadium and through the trophy collection *(Mon–Sat 10am–7pm, Sun 10.30am–6.30pm, on match days up to five hours before kick-off | 19 euros | access via Tower B, tickets at counter 10 by gate 7 on the Paseo de la Castellana* **(125 D3) (ɰ 0))**. At the *Real Café Bernabéu (daily 10am–2am, on match days closed two hours before until one hour after the match | access gate 30 | www.realcafebernabeu.es | Moderate)* you get to dine in style with an enviable view of the soccer field. *Metro 10: Santiago Bernabéu* (*www.horariosenespana. es*) has nothing against a short afternoon nap as such. His criticism is aimed at the 3-hour break which workers in Spain are forced to take between 2pm and 5pm. This long break at midday pushes back the close of the workday, depriving Spaniards of sleep at night and putting additional pressure on family life. Buqueras has yet to record any major success.

to the arena to witness a fight between equals. They want to watch how the torero uses his skills to dominate the bull, who appears at first glance to overpower the torero, and finally kill the animal

Bronze statue of Madrid's emblem at the east side of the Puerta del Sol

TAUROMAQUIA

Tauromaquia is the Spanish word for bullfighting, yet it is not considered a blood sport within the areas where it is practiced. Instead it is seen as a highly ritualized cultural event and art form. Critics however point out that the toreros (bullfighters) do not fight with the bull, they seek only to kill the animal in this ritualized spectacle. The aficionados, or supporters of Tauromaquia, do not come ideally by a single sword thrust. However this atavistic spectacle is losing its popularity in Spain where the bullfighting arenas are struggling to fill even a third of their seats with some almost empty. This waning interest is coupled with political pressure from animal right activists who condemn the ritual killing of the bull as "brutal torture" and "murder". When the Parliament of Catalonia banned bullfighting in the region in 2010, it was seen as a victory for animal rights. However it will take a while before Madrid is ready to end bullfighting. Spain's Conservative majority parliament declared the Tauromaquia to be a "common cultural heritage" in 2013.

SIGHTSEEING

CITY WHERE TO START?
Naturally to **Puerta del Sol** (122–123 C–D 2–3) (*Ⓜ F4)*! The "Gate of the Sun" might not be the prettiest square in Madrid, but the city's central hub where busy office workers and the leisurely, demonstrators and living statues, shoppers and lottery ticket sellers all meet up. Close by is the noble Plaza Mayor (the "main square"), Madrid's showcase square which is overrun by tourists. And then on to Plaza de Santa Ana with its street cafés and mixture of people happily enjoying tapas and *caña*.

Madrid does not have an Eiffel Tower, a Big Ben or a Coliseum. But it does have "Las Meninas" by Velázquez, "Guernica" by Picasso and dozens of other masterpieces from art history. The Prado, the Reina Sofia and the Thyssen-Bornemisza, three of the most important collections of paintings in the world, are all must sees if you visit Madrid.

Apart from that, Spain's capital, city of secret sights, is waiting to be discovered. Madrid's magnificent buildings are less grand than those in other European cities, its churches don't exude the same splendour and its boulevards are a little more modest. That said most visitors to this city take home with them nothing but wonderful

An unhurried approach is the best way to discover Madrid – simply let its streets sweep you along

memories – but when asked what these memories are made of, it is usually difficult for them to pinpoint what makes Madrid so unique.

In fact the whole city is worth seeing but its main attraction is its historic centre. The streets and squares seem to exude harmony and vibrant life. The architecture, dating from the 19th and 20th century, may not be its biggest draw card, yet walking along the rows of houses can be quite uplifting. Do as the locals do: let the city buzz draw you

in, wander around aimlessly, people watch – and before you know it you too discover your own favourite attractions.

What you may notice is that the locals call none of Madrid's *barrios* – its inner city neighbourhoods – by the official names you will find on city maps. The administrative names of central squares, streets or Metro stations have been absorbed by those in everyday use – their real names long forgotten.

The map shows the location of the most interesting districts. There is a detailed map of each district on which each of the sights described is numbered.

SOL, HUERTAS AND RETIRO

In the heart of city – in the heart of Spain – is the Puerta del Sol square in the centre of Madrid. It is also the centre of Spain's long distance road network with a *kilómetro cero* pavement plaque from which a web of national roads feed across the entire country and from which all distances are measured.

South-east of the Puerta del Sol is ★ *Huertas* – the nightlife district popular with tourists and locals alike. The name Huertas means "vegetable gardens" which was initially the name of the main street in the district south-east of the

Puerta del Sol. Before long it was the name of the whole *barrio*. When you visit Huertas your first point of contact will be the *Plaza Santa Ana*. It is surrounded by tavernas, bars and pubs whose outdoor tables are quickly snapped up in good weather.

Huertas has another unofficial name: *Barrio de las Letras* (the neighbourhood of words) because some of the greatest Spanish poets lived and worked here during the *siglo de oro* the "golden" era of the 17th century. Among them Miguel de Cervantes, Félix Lope de Vega, Luis de Góngora and Francisco de Quevedo. The *Casa Museo Lope de Vega* (123 E3) (*∅ G5*) (Tue–Sun 10am–6pm, guided tours every 30 minutes only by appointment at casamuseolopedevega@madrid.

org or tel. 914 29 92 16 | free admission | C/ de Cervantes 11), where the author lived, has been made into a small museum and also has a INSIDER TIP small secluded garden.

The house in which his contemporary Miguel de Cervantes spent the last years of his life was torn down in the first half of the 19th century. The *Convento de las Trinitarias ((123 E4) (⚑ G5) | C/ Lope de Vega 18)* where Cervantes was laid to rest does however still exist. In 2014 the search began for remains in the crypt, the exact location of which had remained unknown for centuries.

1 CAIXAFORUM ★
(123 F4–5) (⚑ G5)

Swiss architects Pierre de Meuron and Jacques Herzog have turned a former coal-fired power station from 1900 into a futuristic, gravity defying cultural centre. Right of the entrance is an eye-catching vertical garden that can best be described as a living painting. The cultural centre of the former Caixa Bank was opened in 2008 and has an extensive programme of exhibitions, readings, films and concerts. *Daily 10am–8pm | admission 4 euros | Paseo del Prado 36 | obrasocial. lacaixa.es | Metro 1: Atocha*

2 MONASTERIO DE LAS DESCALZAS REALES (122 C2) (⚑ E–F4)

Juana de Austria, King Felipe II's sister, founded this Franciscan Convent where today only 19 nuns still live in 1559. A visit to this palace built in the Castilian *Plateresco* style and richly decorated with sacred art (e.g. a series of Rubens tapestries on the Eucharist) is like a journey into the Spanish Renaissance. There is also a rather curious INSIDER TIP collection of Christ child artworks. *Tue–Sat 10am–2pm and 4pm–6.30pm, Sun 10am–3pm | admission 6 euros (not included in Madrid*

Card), free on Wed and Thu afternoons for EU citizens | Plaza de las Descalzas 3 | Metro 3, 5: Callao

3 MUSEO NACIONAL DEL PRADO ★
(123 F3–4) (* illustration* G5)

When architect Juan de Villanueva began construction work on the Prado in 1785 on the instruction of Charles III, King of Spain, he assumed that it would house a Natural History Museum. But his grandson Ferdinand VII decided to exhibit the royal collection of paintings in the finished building from 1819 onwards. Over time, the museum earned its reputation as one of the most important art galleries in the world. The Villanueva building today houses works from the 12th through to the 19th century with the focus on Spanish paintings. The Prado houses the most extensive collection of works by El Greco (1541–1614), Velázquez (1599–1660) and Goya (1746–1828) not to mention those of contemporaries to Velázquez: José de Ribera, Francisco de Zurbarán and Bartolomé Esteban Murillo. Aside from these, there are also some exceptional paintings by Flemish artists Hieronymus Bosch, Rubens and Brueghel, as well as works by Germans Albrecht Dürer and Lucas Cranach, Italians like Botticelli, Rafael, Titian, Tintoretto and Caravaggio that stand out among hundreds more painters.

The museum is the proud owner of some 7600 paintings, 1000 sculptures and more than 8000 sketches. Only a good 1300 works can be displayed. The best way to tackle the Prado is by making a must see list and then getting one's bearings. Prioritising one masterpiece over another may seem unfair but when you take a guided tour these are some of the works you will definitely get to see:

Las Meninas: "The Maids of Honour" by Diego de Velázquez. Art historians are fascinated by the artist's perspective and how he placed himself in the foreground, albeit slightly in its shadows, while the background has the

The popular Prado is rarely this empty

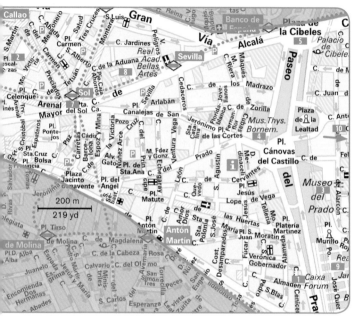

SIGHTSEEING IN SOL, HUERTAS AND RETIRO

1 Caixaforum
2 Monasterio de las
  Descalzas Reales
3 Museo Nacional del Prado
4 Museo Thyssen-Bornemisza

5 Plaza de Cibeles
6 Plaza Mayor
7 Puerta del Sol
8 Real Academia de Bellas Artes
  de San Fernando

▨ Pedestrian precinct
9 Real Jardín Botánico
10 Retiro
11 San Ginés

royal couple Felipe IV and Maria Anna visible in a mirror.

El Jardín de las Delicias: "The Garden of Earthly Delights" by Hieronymus Bosch. The conventional interpretation of the triptych from around 1500 is that for Bosch (El Bosco in Spanish) it was a metaphorical representation of paradise, earthly sinners and the torments of hell. The German art historian Hans Belting has a completely different take on it. He is of the opinion that at the focal point of the painting are the innocent, those in touch with nature and not capable of sin.

Perro semihundido: "The Dog" – by Francisco de Goya. The sight of the sad small dog at the lower section of the painting is one that is not easy to forget. It is one of Goya's later "black paintings". Also take the time to admire his *El tres de Mayo*: "The Third of May" depicting the shootings on 3 May 1808 and the day of the Spanish resistance to Napoleon's occupation; the life-sized group portrait *Charles IV and his Family,* as well as his *Maja Clothed* and *Maja Nude.*
Other highlights: *David with the Head of Goliath* by Caravaggio, *The Three Graces*

SOL, HUERTAS AND RETIRO

by Peter Paul Rubens, *The Annunciation* by Fra Angelico, *Self-portrait* by Albrecht Dürer, and *The Crucifixion* by El Greco.

In 2007 the museum's new east wing extension by architect Rafael Moneo was opened – a light, cool building built around the cloisters of the former monastery. Since then, the Prado's surface area has grown by 50 per cent; the extension is mainly used for special exhibitions. To avoid the queues, it's best to buy online tickets in advance at *www.entradasprado.com. Mon–Sat 10am–8pm, Sun 10am–7pm, 24/31 Dec and 6 Jan 10am–2pm, closed 1 Jan, 1 May and 25 Dec | admission 14 euros, ● Mon–Sat 6–8pm, Sun 5–7pm free | Paseo del Prado | www.museodelprado.es | Metro 1, 2: Atocha, Banco de España*

▣ MUSEO THYSSEN-BORNEMISZA ★
(123 F3) (*ᗝ G4*)

Friedrich Thyssen, second-born son of August Thyssen had no interest in his father's business – the founding father of the iron and steel empire in Germany's industrial Ruhr area – and married a Hungarian baroness by the name of Bornemisza, an art collector. Their son Hans-Heinrich (1921–2002) became a Swiss citizen and also took an interest in art adding to their original collection works by German Expressionists. At the time of his death he had collected some 1500 works. It was a collection that read like the A to Z of European and North American art history. The central part of the collection, some 800 paintings, are displayed in this museum housed in the 18th century Palacio Villahermosa with an extension that displays a further 220 paintings.

For a chronological walk through the art from the 13th to 20th century, you will start on the second floor and end on the ground floor. Standing out: *Giovanna Tornabuoni* (1488) by Domenico Ghirlandaio, *Henry VIII* (1534) by Hans Holbein the Younger, *Portrait of a Young Man* (1515) by Raffael. There is also Edgar Degas' *Swaying Dancer* (1877–79). *Mon noon–4pm, Tue–Sun 10am–7pm | admis-*

UNUSUAL SHOPS

The Antigua Farmacia de la Reina Madre (122 B3) (*ᗝ E4–5*) (*C/ Mayor 59*) is an interesting old chemist's shop that is packed to its carved wooden ceiling with earthen pots. The *Almacén de Pontejos* (122 C3) (*ᗝ F4*) (*Plaza de Pontejos 2*) is a haberdashery that sells every conceivable sewing item including buttons, zips, lace or embroidery patterns in every colour and style. *Capas Seseña* (123 D3) (*ᗝ F5*) (*C/ de la Cruz 23*) specialises exclusively in tailor-made capes. These sleeveless merino wool garments were not only popular in Goya's and Velázquez's times, Hillary Clinton and Oliver Stone are also among its customers. The *Antigua Casa Crespo* (127 F3) (*ᗝ F3*) (*C/ Divino Pastor 29*), founded in 1863, is a fourth generation run business that sells Spanish alpargatas – the traditional Spanish espadrilles with hemp soles – as well as woven baskets made from esparto grass. *Caramelos Paco* (122 B4) (*ᗝ E5*) (*C/ Toledo 55*) is a children's paradise that has been around since 1936: its shop window is bursting with sweets.

The ornately decorated Palacio de Cibeles stands behind the Cybele fountain on Plaza de Cibeles

sion 10 euros, Mon free | Paseo del Prado 8 | www.museothyssen.org | Metro 2: Banco de España

5 PLAZA DE CIBELES ★
(123 F2) *(M G4)*

Lacking an official emblem, the Fuente de la Cibeles serves as Madrid's unofficial one. Cybele was an Asia Minor goddess who was also revered in Rome as the mother of nature. In Madrid, she has been sitting in her lion-drawn carriage on this square, today named after her and surrounded by heavy traffic, since 1782. The Madrilenos love their goddess. During the Spanish civil war, they hid the statue under a pyramid of sand bags and bricks. Today Cybele has to be protected from her most avid fans, the supporters and players of Real Madrid who celebrate their victories around the fountain.

The main attraction on th square is the Another attraction on the square is the *Palacio de Cibeles*, built in 1917 and designed by the then star architect Antonio Palacios. The former central post office today houses the city's administration as well as the civic and culture centre ● *Centro Centro* (www.centrocentro.org). From the *Mirador (Tue–Sun 10.30am–1.30pm and 4–7pm | admission 2 euros)*, city and plaza lie at your feet. Making up the other three corners of the square are the *Banco de España* (Spain's central bank), the *Palacio de Buenavista* (seat of the Spanish Armed Forces) and the *Casa de América* (Latin American Cultural Centre). 200 m/656 ft further eastwards on Calle de Alcalá you will find the triumphal arch *Puerta de Alcalá*. The Spanish king Charles III set up a memorial to himself here at the end of the 18th century. *Metro 2: Banco de España*

6 PLAZA MAYOR ★
(122 B–C3) *(M E4–5)*

This is Madrid's main square and the pace here is slower than elsewhere in the city with everyone taking time out to enjoy the restaurant *terrazas* and listen to the buskers. In the centre of the plaza, around the equestrian statue of Felipe III, groups of young tourists congregate to chat, laze in the sun or play the guitar. Amateur caricature artists set up their easels in front of the arcades waiting for business.

In the Middle Ages this was the location of the Plaza del Arrabal, the main market square, just outside the city allegorical paintings on its façade are more recent and are from 1992.

You should take a walk down the romantic *Escalerilla de Piedra* stone staircase in the south-western corner of the square. It takes you down to the Cava San Miguel. Once on the street look back to admire the massive walls of the residential homes that line the western edge of the square where there is one

The murals on the Casa de la Panadería at the Plaza Mayor were painted in 1992

gates. In 1619 the Plaza Mayor was formed as a rectangular shape, but what you see here today was largely rebuilt from 1790 onwards after several devastating fires. The Plaza Mayor was also once the scene of auto-da-fés (the Inquisition's heretic courts and burnings at the stake) and for folk festivals or bullfights. Over on the northern side of the square is the *Casa de la Panadería,* an old granary once used by the city's bread bakers. Today it houses the tourist information. The restaurant after another. The *Botín (daily | C/ de los Cuchilleros 17 | tel. 913 66 42 17 | Expensive)* opened its doors in 1725 and calls itself the world's oldest restaurant. Its speciality is *cochinillo,* suckling pig. *Metro 1, 2, 3: Sol*

7 PUERTA DEL SOL
(122–123 C–D 2–3) (⊞ F4)

Nos vemos en el Oso y el Madroño: "Let's meet at the bear and the strawberry tree". The statue of city's unusual emblem that marks the entrance to the Calle de Alcalá serves as a meeting place for everyone who couldn't think of a better one. Especially in the evening you will see dozens of people hanging around here waiting for someone. Once everyone is found, they'll head away – no one stays on the Puerta del Sol. It is a square to pass through, a square everyone working in the inner city has to cross. On the northern side of the big semicircle, Madrid's oldest neon sign advertises Tío Pepe Sherry. On the western end, the Café Mallorquina has been serving coffees and pastries since 1894. The unusual bell tower of the *Casa de Correos* on the southern side of the square comes into its own once a year when New Year's Eve is celebrated. The former central post office building now houses regional government offices. During the Franco dictatorship political opponents were tortured in its cellars.

To the left and right of the main entrance are two plaques, one commemorates the heroes of the 2 May 1808 uprising against Napoleon and another commemorates the helpers of the 11 March 2004 terror attack. Pedestrians and tourists can often be seen staring down at the ground outside the Casa de Correos where there is a plaque marking Spain's Kilometre Zero, the point from which Spain's network of six major highways is measured. *Metro 1, 2, 3: Sol*

8 INSIDER TIP REAL ACADEMIA DE BELLAS ARTES DE SAN FERNANDO (123 D2) (*m F4*)

The museum functions as the Royal Academy of Fine Arts established by royal decree in 1752. Although the gallery does not draw in large crowds, it houses a fine modest collection of important paintings from El Greco, Diego de Velázquez, Alonso Cano, Arcimboldo and Peter Paul Rubens with its main attraction of 13 Goyas, including one of his self-portraits painted when he was 69. *Tue–Sun 10am–3pm | admission 6 euros | C/ de Alcalá 13 | www.realacademiabellasartes sanfernando.com | Metro 2: Sevilla*

9 REAL JARDÍN BOTÁNICO (123 F4–5) (*m G5*)

More than 200 years ago, in 1781, Charles III established the botanical gardens right next to the Prado, and some of its 30,000 trees are now more than 200 years old. Visitors can admire shrubs and flowers from around the world, as well as the **INSIDER TIP** bonsai collection of former Prime Minister Felipe González. *Daily*

KEEP FIT!

When you've had your share of being indoors after all those hours spent in the museums, then it is time to do as the locals do and head for the Retiro. You can go for a jog or you can also check out *La Chopera* **(132 C1)** (*m H5*) *(Mon–Fri 8.30am–8.45pm, Sat/Sun 8.30am–2.30pm | admission 5 euros)*, with soccer, tennis and body building facilities The extensive *Casa de Campo* green belt is also a good option for a stroll or jog. Then there is ● Madrid's most beautiful public swimming pool at the edge of the forest which is open from June to August **(126 A6)** (*m B4*) *(daily 11am–8.30pm | admission 6 euros | Paseo Puerta del Ángel 7 | Metro 10: Lago)*.

10am–dusk | admission 3 euros | Plaza Murillo 2 | www.rjb.csic.es | Metro 1: Atocha

10 RETIRO ⭐ (128–129 C–D 5–6, 132–133 C–D 1–2) (𝄞 H–J 4–5)

A clear blue spring sky, the perfect time of year. You will see entire extended families (and their dogs) take the time for a stroll in the urban park, the Retiro. A loving couple on a rowing boat adds to the idyllic setting and as you get closer to the paved shore of the artificial lake the sound of a saxophone floats through the air. A woman carries on feeding her loaf of stale bread to the pigeons. An elegant palm reader seated at his makeshift table telling his first customer their fortune. At the other side of the lake, beneath the mighty *equestrian statue of Alfons XII,* some youngsters laze in the sun smoking a joint quite openly.

Tourists are drawn into the centre of the park to the renovated ● *Palacio de Cristal (free admission)* and ● *Palacio de Velázquez (free admission)* with their collections of contemporary art. In the south of the park is the unique *Fuente del Ángel Caído* – probably the only statue of Lucifer in the whole world. In the south-west of the park the *Bosque de los Ausentes*, comprising 192 Cyprus and olive trees, is a tribute to the victims of the terror attack of 11 March 2004 when Islamist extremists blew up four commuter trains heading to Madrid.

In the 17th century the Spanish king, Felipe IV established the Parque del Buen Retiro or "park of the pleasant retreat" as a royal garden. It has been open to the general public since 1868 – a green oasis that tuurns into a village fair on weekends. *April–Sept daily 6am–midnight, Oct–March 6am–10pm | Metro 1, 2, 9: Retiro, Ibiza, Atocha*

11 SAN GINÉS (122 C2) (𝄞 E4)

This small baroque church houses an absolute gem: El Greco's "Christ Driving the Money Changers from the Temple" (1610–1614), the most impressive painting you can see in Madrid without being in a museum. *Guided visits Sat 10am–11am and 11.30am–noon | free admission | C/ de Arenal 13 | Metro 1, 2, 3, 5: Sol, Ópera*

MADRID DE LOS AUSTRIAS/ LA LATINA

⭐ **This neighbourhood owes its unofficial name to the Habsburgs, who came to the Spanish throne with Charles V in the 16th century, before they were replaced by the Bourbons at the beginning of the 18th century after the Spanish War of Succession.**

It was the Austrian Habsburgs that made Madrid Spain's capital in the mid 16th century. They left very little of the old medieval city and today there are a few traces left in the Madrid de los Austrias. The area surrounding the Royal Palace and its alleyways in the south-east has retained the kind of charm that is hard to find in the rest of Madrid. This can probably be ascribed to the way its narrow medieval streets, filled with rows of houses, all seem to tumble downhill in a charming jumble. To the left and right of Calle Segovia between Puerta Cerrada and the Viaducto is where you will experience this district at its most captivating and it is hard to imagine that this sleepy *barrio* turns into a bustling *zona de marcha* at night. The in-crowd has given the suburb its own name: La Latina – named after the closest Metro station.

1 CALLE MAYOR
(122 A–C3) (*E–F4*)

What was once the main road of medieval Madrid is today a vibrant residential, office and shopping street in the heart of the city, with beautifully restored buildings such as the *Edificio de la Compañía Colonial* (number 16/18) with its art nouveau façade dating back to 1909. The quiet, almost inconspicuous *Plaza de la Villa* is located at the south end of the road where Madrid's former city hall, the *Casa de la Villa* dating to the 17th century, once stood. Opposite is the *Casa y Torre de los Lujanes,* an aristocratic palace that dates back to the 15th century, making it Madrid's oldest secular building with a horseshoe arch serving as the entrance gate. *Metro 1, 2, 3, 5: Sol, Ópera*

2 INSIDER TIP CAMPO DEL MORO ●
(127 D6) (*D4*)

This elegant park behind the Palacio Real with its expansive lawns is not that popular with the citizens of Madrid. This may be because it is not that easy to reach. From the Royal Palace you take the narrow pavement path downhill along the busy Cuesta de San Vicente. Those of you who decide to venture there (it is more comfortable to take the Metro) will find that you have the park almost entirely to yourself. The park also has the *Fuente de las Conchas* – a fountain with three statues of children holding a huge shell to their mouth, while a fourth child hugs a dolphin. *April–Sept daily 10am–8pm, Oct–March 10am–6pm, closed on official occasions | Metro 6, 10: Príncipe Pío*

3 CATEDRAL DE LA ALMUDENA
(122 A3) (*D4–5*)

Inaugurated only in 1993 Madrid's neo-classical cathedral is a contemporary building, and few residents were pleased with it. Nevertheless they have now taken their cathedral a little more to heart – especially after then Crown Prince Felipe de Borbón y Grecia married his Letizia here in 2004. If you visit the cathedral museum

The eye-catching, pompous statue of King Alfonso XII on his horse at the Estanque in the Retiro park

(Mon–Sat 10am–2.30pm | 6 euros | museocatedral.archimadrid.es), you can also see the sacristy, the chapter house and the dome *Daily 9am–8.30pm | free admission | Bailén 10 | Metro 2, 5: Ópera*

🟦 PALACIO REAL ⭐
(122 A2) (𝄞 D4)

In the mid 18th century Italian architects were tasked with designing a new palace that would bring the grandeur of Versailles to Madrid. Despite their brief, Felipe V's Palacio Real ended up being a very Spanish construction: serious, square and powerful. Baroque splendour prevails on the noble three of its seven floors: 24 acres of the royal household's interior floor space. As a visitor you will be whisked through 50 of the 280 royal rooms in the space of an hour, transporting you into an unreal world of precious paintings, tapestries, ceiling frescoes, ornaments, chandeliers, furniture, clocks, crockery, swords, armour, maps and books – and last but not least the royal pharmacy.

After the old Alcázar burned down here in 1734, construction work began in earnest using the classical architectural designs of Italians Filippo Juvarra and Giovanni Battista Sacchetti. Charles III became the first occupant in 1764 and it remained the Palacio Real or Royal Palace until the monarchy was overthrown in 1931. Since its reinstitution in 1975, the Royal Family lives outside of Madrid in the Palacio de la Zarzuela. From October to June, the INSIDER TIP solemn changing of the guard is performed on the first Wednesday of each month at 12 noon in front of the Palacio Real. *April–Sept daily 10am–8pm, Oct–March 10am–6pm | admission 11 euros, ⬤ Mon–Thu free for EU citizens in the last two hours before closure | C/Bailén | www.patrimonionacional.es | Metro 2, 5: Ópera*

King Felipe V liked opulence – the Palacio Real in all its splendour

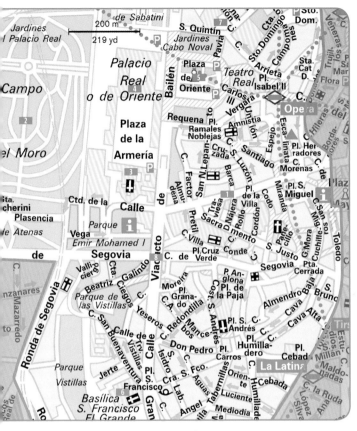

SIGHTSEEING IN MADRID DE LOS AUSTRIAS/LA LATINA

▨ Pedestrian precinct

1 Calle Mayor
2 Campo del Moro
3 Catedral de la Almudena
4 Palacio Real
5 Plaza de Oriente
6 Real Basílica de
  San Francisco el Grande
7 Real Monasterio
  de la Encarnación
8 Viaducto

5 PLAZA DE ORIENTE
(122 A2) (*Ø E4*)

A fittingly noble square between the Palacio Real and the Teatro Real, Madrid's opera house. José Bonaparte, appointed by his brother Napoleon as the King of Spain in 1808, gave the order to build the square. José, who was used to the wide open spaces of Paris, found Madrid's narrow streets to be oppressive. He tore down many homes and churches to make room for the city square, but in the end the crescent shaped Plaza de Oriente was only completed by the Bourbon

The magnificent 72 m/236 ft high dome of the Basílica de San Francisco el Grande

Queen Isabella II. The Visigoth statues that surround the green inner square were originally supposed to adorn the palace balustrade.

Underworld Madrid can also be fascinating. Descend the flight of stairs at the junction with the Calle Felipe V until you reach the parking level then take a few steps to the right where a glass panel protects the foundations of an *atalaya*, a watchtower from the Islamic period (11th century) – one of the few intact remains of medieval Madrid. *Metro 2, 5: Ópera*

▇ REAL BASÍLICA DE SAN FRANCISCO EL GRANDE (122 A5) (🏛 D5)

This is Madrid's most art historically significant church. It was built in the neoclassical style (1761–68) with a 33 m/108 ft wide, 72 m/236 ft high vaulted dome. Inside in the side chapels there are paintings by Spanish artists from the late 19th century as well as works by Zurbarán,

Cano and Goya. *Sept–June Tue–Sat 10.30am–12.30pm and 4pm–6pm, July/Aug Tue–Sun 10.30am–12.30pm and 5pm–7pm | admission 3 euros | San Buenaventura 1 | Metro 5: La Latina*

▇ REAL MONASTERIO DE LA ENCARNACIÓN (122 A–B 1–2) (🏛 E4)

It's worth visiting this slightly indulging convent of the order of Recolet Augustines (founded in 1611) for its INSIDER TIP room of reliquaries housing over 700 ornately decorated shrines made of bronze, ivory, coral and precious wood containing holy remains of bones, snippets of hair, fabrics and splinters of wood. The most famous reliquary is one that contains the blood of San Pantaleón, which purportedly liquefies in the church each year on 27 July. *Tue–Sat 10am–2pm and 4pm–6.30pm, Sun 10am–3pm | admission 6 euros | Plaza de la Encarnación 1 | Metro 2, 5: Ópera, Santo Domingo*

8 VIADUCTO ⚜

(122 A3–4) (𝖔 D–E5)

Back in the 18th century the architect Giovanni Battista Sacchetti dreamt of a way to link "his" Palacio Real with the Basílica San Francisco el Grande by a bridge but it was only in 1874 that an iron viaduct made the dream become a reality. In 1942 it was replaced by a reinforced concrete bridge in a style reminiscent of 1761–68. For a time it gained notoriety for its suicides (Segovia street is 25 m/82 feet below, which is why the bridge is also called "Viaducto de Segovia"), but today there is a 2 m/6.5 ft high glass protective plate. Southwest of the Viaducto lies the ⚜ *Jardines de las Vistillas,* a small park where you can enjoy some peace and quiet and spectacular views of the Sierra de Guadarrama mountains in the distance, preferably with a glass of *tinto de verano* on the terrace of the *Restaurante El Ventorrillo. Metro 2, 5: Ópera, La Latina*

CHUECA, MALASAÑA AND CONDE DUQUE

Chueca is Madrid's gay district. You will find a hip, young, fashionable and colourful nightlife scene in the streets around Fuencarral, Gran Vía, Recoletos and Calle.

Until the 1990s the central Plaza Chueca was a grim meeting place for dealers and junkies and it is thanks to the gay community in this neighbourhood that the area was transformed. They bought and renovated homes and as a spin-off lots of chic shops and restaurants opened. All of a sudden, Chueca was a hip nightlife quarter, for hetero- as well as for homosexual people. Also benefiting from this upturn was *Calle de Fuencarral,* which marks the western border of the district. Today it is the liveliest shopping precinct in Madrid.

Salon on the Calle de Fuencarral shopping boulevard in trendy Chueca

Malasaña, the area west of Calle de Fuencarral, once had almost as bad a reputation as Chueca did in the 1980s. But by the end of the 20th century the rehabilitation of the suburb made Madrid's dubious crowd lose interest in it. The name of this district goes back to a young heroine of the Madrid uprising against the French on 2 May 1808. This date is commemorated with the *Plaza Dos de Mayo,* the cosy heart of the neighbourhood. Malasaña remains a favourite choice for the nightly *zonas de marcha* of the young crowd and students. At the same time more and more shops and restaurants are opening their doors here during the day, drawing folk from all over the city, e.g. in the area around Calle Ballesta called *Triball,* which stands for Triángulo (triangle) Ballesta and where there are still a few prostitutes waiting for clients.

Boutiques and interesting shops can also be found scattered around the otherwise quiet section surrounding the Conde Duque cultural centre. This historic old residential area is full of cosy pubs, tapas bars and *terrazas.* In the west it joins up with Malasaña.

■ CASA LONGORIA
(128 B4) (*G3*)

With the completion of this house in 1903, the Catalonian architect José Grases Riera brought his own personal interpretation of Catalan Modernism – a Spanish variant of art nouveau – to Madrid. The building was commissioned by Javier González Longoria, a banker and politician. The building's excessive façade is the subject of much debate while its interior spiral staircase with its iron, bronze and marble features has a timeless appeal. The Spanish authors' association (SGAE) is housed here today. *C/ Fernando VI 4, corner Pelayo 61 | Metro 4, 5, 10: Alonso Martínez*

■ GRAN VÍA
(122–123 B–E 1–2) (*E3–4, F4*)

"If you only have a few hours to spend in Madrid, I'd always recommend a walk

The Telefónica headquarters from 1929: the highest building along Madrid's grand boulevard, the Gran Vía

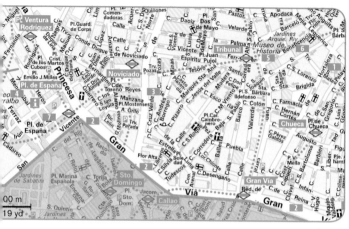

SIGHTSEEING IN CHUECA, MALASAÑA AND CONDE DUQUE

▨ Pedestrian precinct

1 Casa Longoria
2 Gran Vía
3 Julia

4 Museo Cerralbo
5 Museo de Historia de Madrid

6 Museo del Romanticismo
7 Plaza de España
8 Templo de Debod

down the Gran Vía", said the film director Pablo Berger. "You get all walks of life here, from bankers to prostitutes, locals dashing to their destinations, tourists wandering aimlessly around, shoppers, beggars and pickpockets: it's Madrid's real-life zoo." Built at the start of the 20th century, this 1.3 km/0.8 mile, six-lane road cut an incision into Madrid's old town. The buildings are higher on the Gran Via than most in Madrid's centre with an eclectic style of belle-époque facades, sculptures and roof pillars as well as U.S.-style skyscrapers. The boulevard's highest building is the old Telefónica headquarters (1929) with its blue lit clock dominating the city's skyline.

The appeal of the Gran Vía is its proximity to the authentic, more traditional Madrid. Pablo Berger sums up the street's charm: "You walk down the long avenida with its splendid buildings, offices, hotels and boutiques and just a few metres fur-

ther, down one of its side streets away from the fashion stores and fast-food chains, you'll encounter a señora in her dressing gown and slippers. Village life in the big city. I don't think you'll find such a contrast on such a compact space in any of the world's other capitals." *Metro 1, 5: Gran Vía*

3 INSIDER TIP JULIA (127 F4) (*Ø E3*)

A young woman wearing a skirt and blouse, leaning casually against the wall, with one leg slightly raised, holding a book in her right hand: This bronze statue belongs to Malasaña like the Little Mermaid does to Copenhagen. The artist, Antonio Santín, heard about the "strange case of Doncella Julia", the story of a young woman, who dressed up as a boy in the 1840s in order to attend classes at Madrid University, a privilege which until 1910 was only open to men in Spain. Inspired by this anecdote and using a pretty fellow student as a model, Santín created this figure for Madrid's old university district who he named Julia. *C/ del Pez/C/ San Bernardo | Metro 2: Noviciado*

▟ MUSEO CERRALBO
(127 D4) (*ℳ D3*)

In this palace that the 17th Marqués de Cerralbo (1845–1922) turned into a museum himself and bequeathed to Spain after his death in 1922, time is standing still. Medals, weapons, watches, artworks from all epochs, chandeliers, porcelain, furniture, tapestries: the collection of a nobleman in the taste of the late 19th century. *Tue–Sat 9.30am–3pm, Thu also 5pm–8pm, Sun 10am–3pm | admission 3 euros, ● Sat 2pm–3pm and Sun free admission | C/ Ventura Rodríguez 17 | museocerralbo.mcu.es | Metro 3, 10: Plaza de España*

▜ MUSEO DE HISTORIA DE MADRID
(128 A4) (*ℳ F3*)

Madrid's 18th century hospital now hoouses the city museum. The splendour of its baroque entrance portal is quite overwhelming. Learn more about the history of Madrid from the paintings (among them Goyas *Alegoría de la Villa de Madrid),* photos and documents and the museum's highlight an INSIDER TIP ▶ exact replica of Madrid in the year 1830. *Tue–Sun 11am–2pm and 4pm–7pm | free admission | C/ de Fuencarral 78 | Metro 1, 10: Tribunal*

▞ MUSEO DEL ROMANTICISMO
(128 A4) (*ℳ F3*)

Entering this seemingly unassuming palace (built in 1776) for the first time feels like you are secretly visiting a private salon from the 19th century. Alongside a treasure trove of furniture, bric-a-brac and musical instruments, the museum also houses paintings of some lesser-known Spanish Romanticist artists. It offers a terrific opportunity to discover painters such as Federico Madrazo or Antonio María Esquivel. After a visit, enjoy a cup of tea at the *Café del Jardín,* the museum's garden café. *Tue–Sat 9.30am–8.30pm (Nov–April until 6.30pm), Sun 10am–3pm | admission 3 euros, Sat from 2pm free admission | C/ San Mateo 13 | museoromanticismo.mcu. es | Metro 1, 10: Tribunal*

▟ PLAZA DE ESPAÑA
(127 D–E 4–5) (*ℳ D–E3*)

This large square at the western end of the Gran Vía is surrounded on all sides by an uninterrupted flow of traffic and flanked by some rather drab, functional buildings. However, Madrid's city slickers still meet up here, undeterred by the city noise. Gracing the centre of the square (since 1928) is Spain's fictional national hero

Don Quixote mounted on his steed Rosinante, with his trusted squire Sancho Panza beside him. Behind them is Miguel de Cervantes, looking down sternly on his literary characters. Prominent buildings are the 25-storey *Edificio de España* on the square's north-east side, that dates back to 1953 (currently standing empty) and alongside it the *Torre de Madrid,* a 142 m/466 ft residential tower completed in 1957. *Metro 3, 10: Plaza de España*

⑧ TEMPLO DE DEBOD ☼
(127 D4) *(⑰ D3)*

This small Egyptian temple devoted to the gods Amun Ra and Isis dates back to the second century BC and is the oldest building in Madrid. However it is only since 1972 that it can be admired at its present location in the southern part of the Parque del Oeste. The temple was a gift from the Egyptian government for Spain's archaeological efforts to save Abu Simbel on the western Nile banks during the building of the Aswan Dam in the 1960s. You get a wonderful view of the Casa de Campo and the Royal Palace from the Templo de Debod – INSIDER TIP it is the best place in Madrid to watch the sunset. *April–Sept Tue–Fri 10am–2pm and 6pm–8pm, Sat/Sun 9.30am–8pm, Oct–March Tue–Fri 9.45am–1.45pm and 4.15pm–6.15pm, Sat/Sun 9.30am–8pm | free admission | C/ Ferraz 1 | Metro 3: Ventura Rodríguez*

LAVAPIÉS AND RASTRO

This neighbourhood has the highest number of foreigners in Madrid – 40 per cent

Spain's national heroes, Don Quixote and Sancho Panza, on the Plaza de España

LAVAPIÉS AND RASTRO

– giving it its **strong anti-establishment and Bohemian atmosphere.**

The *Plaza Lavapiés* has become the living room (as it were) for immigrants from Latin America, North and sub-Saharan Africa. From there, the *Calle de Argumosa* turns off towards the east, largely populated by pubs and restaurants with a mainly young and predominantly Spanish clientele. If you walk further down the street, you'll eventually get to the Reina Sofía museum of modern art that houses Picasso's *Guernica.* From there it is only a few steps to the Estación de Atocha – the train station with its foyer full of tropical plants.

The area to the west of Lavapiés, around the Calle Embajadores and the Plaza Cascorro, is quite run down. It is here where the Rastro, Madrid's large flea market, takes place every Sunday morning. Anyone with a spirit for discovery is bound to find some of the most amazing antique shops here. Lavapiés and the area surrounding the Rastro are neighbourhoods that care little about what the rest of Madrid think.

LOW BUDGET

The city's three top museums – Prado, Reina Sofía and Thyssen-Bornemisza – sell the *Abono Paseo del Arte,* a 25.60 euro ticket that gives you access to all three museums, saving you 6.40 euros.

Do not forget to carry your identity card or passport with you in Madrid: many museums and other institutes offer substantial discounts for pensioners and free admission for EU citizens at certain times of the day.

■ COLEGIATA DE SAN ISIDRO
(122 C4) (*ᨏ E5*)

Madrid's massive baroque cathedral was completed in 1664. For more than a century it served as Madrid's provisional cathedral: from 1885 – when Madrid broke away from Toledo as an independent diocese – to the day of the consecration of Madrid's Almudena in 1993. The building has housed the remains of Madrid's patron saint San Isidro since 1769. *C/ de Toledo 37 | Metro 5: La Latina*

■ ESTACIÓN DE ATOCHA ★ ●
(123 F6) (*ᨏ G–H6*)

The outside may look like a railway station but inside it feels like a tropical greenhouse. For at least a century locomotives would chug into the spectacular station beneath the arched iron and glass roof,

The Estación de Atocha's wonderful transformation – train station as tropical garden

until the Spanish government decided that a high-speed train was what was needed for the 1992 Expo in Seville. For the state-of-the-art train, known as the *AVE*, a new hall was designed by architect Rafael Moneo, built directly behind the old, making room for a conservatory inside the train station. The resultant palm garden is best enjoyed from the *Samarkanda (daily | tel. 915 30 97 46 | Moderate)* – a restaurant on an elevated terrace on the north side of the lobby.

On the morning of 11 March 2004 Islamic terrorists set off ten bombs on four suburban trains killing 191 people. One of the *cercanías* or suburban trains had just entered the Estación de Atocha. Today a glass memorial on the eastern side of the station commemorates the victims. *Metro 1: Atocha Renfe*

▣ MUSEO NACIONAL CENTRO DE ARTE REINA SOFÍA ★ ●
(123 F5–6) (*∅ G6*)

Housed in the former Hospital General designed in the 18th century by the architect Francisco Sabatini, the Reina Sofía follows on chronologically from the Prado (and the gallery is only a few steps away). Since 1992 the centre has exhibited one of the most premier collections of contemporary, mainly Spanish art which spans the 20th century up to now. Its pièce de résistance is Picasso's *Guernica* (second floor, hall 206.06), which the artist painted in 1937 during the Spanish Civil War. It was commissioned by the republican government for the Paris World Exhibition. On 26 April 1937 aircraft of the German Condor Legion dropped their bombs on to the

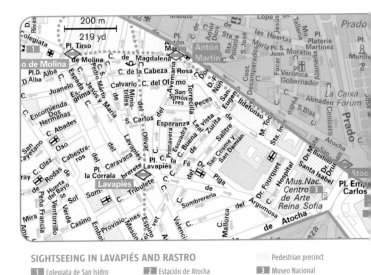

SIGHTSEEING IN LAVAPIÉS AND RASTRO

1 Colegiata de San Isidro **2** Estación de Atocha

▨ Pedestrian precinct

3 Museo Nacional
Centro de Arte Reina Sofía

Basque town of Guernica, destroying three-quarters of the town and killing hundreds of people. It was the first time that the German military on the side of Franco had engaged in total onslaught using the civilian population as its target. An angry and indignant Picasso painted a very explicit scene of the horrors of war. The second floor, alongside Picasso, houses other classical avantgarde works fro the first half of the 20th century, among them wirks by Juan Gris, Francis Picabia, Joan Miró and Salvador Dalí. Take your time to watch the **INSIDER TIP** 16-minute film *Un chien Andalou* by Buñuel and Dalí from 1929 in Hall 203, the peak of surrealist filmmaking. A revelation in Hall 207: the ironic self-portrait *Autorretrato* by Alfonso Ponce de León. The fourth floor is devotes to more recent art, e.g. by Antoni Tàpies, Eduardo Chillida and Antonio López. In 2005 the French architect Jean Nouvel expanded the art museum with a gleaming, bordeaux-red extension that wants to stand out, angering some critics. It makes additional space for temporary exhibitions, a café and restaurant, a library and an exquisite bookstore for art, culture and design.

Mon and Wed–Sat 10am–9pm, Sun 10am–7pm | admission 8 euros, Mon and Wed–Sat from 7pm, Sun from 1.30 pm free | C/ de Santa Isabel 52 | www.museoreinasofia.es | Metro 1: Atocha

SALAMANCA AND CHAMBERÍ

The residents of Madrid's chic and expensive Salamanca barrio are lucky to be living the good life.

Nowhere in Madrid is housing as expensive as in this neighbourhood east of the Paseo de la Castellana and north of the Retiro. This network of roads at right angles is where you will find the city's 19th century urban palaces and elegant townhouses. The areas well-heeled residents are drawn here by its dignified atmosphere and its peaceful nightlife. For visitors to Madrid the Salamanca neighbourhood is of interest primarily because of its exclusive shops on and around the Calle de Serrano and for its fine dining restaurants. To the west of Salamanca,

1 INSIDER TIP MUSEO ANDÉN 0 (128 A–B2) (*M G2*)

A journey back in time and one that goes into the bowels of the city: the old Chamberí station (between the Iglesia and Bilbao stations) was inaugurated by King Alfonso XIII in 1919 and was one of Madrid's first Metro lines. It was however shut down in the 1960s. After having been forgotten for decades it is now a museum where you can see the tiled advertisements for the old bars and shops that once traded here. *Fri 11am–1pm and 5pm–7pm, Sat/Sun 10am–2pm | free admission |*

Exclusive fashion labels are located in the upscale Salamanca district around the Calle de Serrano

on the other side of the Paseo de la Castellana, is Chamberí, a beautiful residential neighbourhood for people for whom money is no object, although with less of the class awareness. It also has some popular down-to-earth places like the *Plaza Chamberí (128 A–B 2) (M G2)* and especially the *Plaza Olavide (128 A2) (M F2)* which has a vibrant nightlife in the summer.

Plaza de Chamberí | Metro 1, 4: Iglesia, Bilbao

2 MUSEO ARQUEOLÓGICO NACIONAL (128 C4) (*M H3*)

Every Spaniard knows about the "Lady of Elche", a stone bust from pre-Roman times found in an archaeological dig near the town of Elche on the Mediterranean near Valencia. Today the

SALAMANCA AND CHAMBERÍ

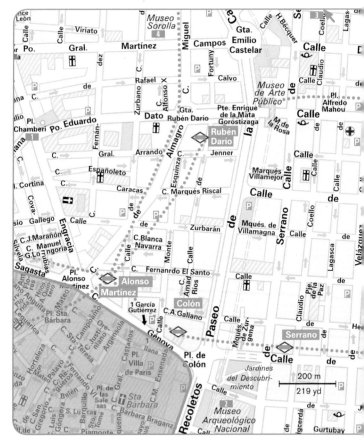

SIGHTSEEING IN SALAMANCA AND CHAMBERÍ

1 Museo Andén 0
2 Museo Arqueológico Nacional
3 Museo Lázaro Galdiano
4 Museo Sorolla

stone statue is displayed in Madrid's national archaeological museum. The museum also houses a collection of Visigoth crowns and gold jewellery. The Germanic tribes, who controlled the Iberian Peninsula (after the Romans) up to the Arab conquest in 711, left behind very little evidence of their culture. *Tue–Sat* *9.30am–8pm, Sun 9.30am–3pm | admission 3 euros | C/ de Serrano 13 | www.man. es | Metro 2, 4: Retiro, Serrano*

3 INSIDER TIP MUSEO LÁZARO GALDIANO (128–129 C–D1) (*∅ H1*)

This hidden treasure in the north of the Salamanca district has yet to be discovered by many of Madrid locals. It houses the astonishing private collection of businessman and publisher José Lázaro Galdiano (1862–1947) including Hieronymus Bosch's "Saint John the Baptist in the Desert" which is itself worth the visit. Other highlights include works by Goya, El Greco, Zurbarán, Velázquez and Lucas Cranach as well as jewellery, weapons, ceramics and furniture from all periods. *Mon and Wed–Sat 10am–4.30pm, Sun 10am–3pm | admission 6 euros, free 1 hr before closing time | C/ de Serrano 122 | www.flg.es | Metro 5: Rubén Darío*

sion 3 euros, Sat from 2pm and Sun free | Paseo General Martinez Campos 37 | museosorolla.mcu.es | Metro 5, 7, 10: Gregorio Maranon, Rubén Darío

MORE SIGHTS

INSIDER TIP ▶ EL CAPRICHO DE LA ALAMEDA DE OSUNA (0) (*0*)

The small park in the east of the city has French, Italian and English influences and is a veritable oasis of peace and tranquil-

Furniture and paintings: the lesser known Museo Lázaro Galdiano

4 MUSEO SOROLLA
(128 B1–2) (*G1*)

This mansion dating from the early 20th century was the home and studio of the Spanish painter Joaquin Sorolla (1863–1923) during the last years of his life. Admire this master's play on water and light to get a real feel for the world he lived in. Lovely Andalusian garden. *Tue–Sat 9.30am–8pm, Sun 10am–3pm | admis-*

lity – dogs, cyclists, soccer games and the like are prohibited. It is a popular setting for wedding photographs. *Only open weekends and public holidays | Metro 5: El Capricho*

CASA DE CAMPO
(126 A–B 5–6) (*A–B 2–4*)

"Country house" is what the name of this park means. Felipe II added one of these to his hunting lodge on the western border of the city in the mid 16th century but it was not until 1931 that the accompanying royal hunting ground was declared open to the public. Today the 3840 acre pine forest is Madrid's green belt, even if its hilly terrain and sparse scattering of trees is very different to the forests you usually find in central Europe. Most visitors tend to make a beeline for the zoo and the *Parque de Atracciones* on the south-eastern border of the Casa de Campo.

An all-time favourite among Madrid's residents is a Sunday excursion on the ⚡ *Teleférico de Madrid* (see p. 105), a cable car that takes you from the southern end of the *Parque del Oeste* (126 C3) *(ﾉﾉ C2)* up to 40 m/131 ft above ground for a distance of 2.5 km/1.5 mile into the Casa de Campo making for excellent views of the park and the city. *Metro 10: Lago*

EL ESCORIAL (134 A1) *(ﾉﾉ 0)*

The royal monastery and palace Real Monasterio de San Lorenzo de El Escorial stands as testimony to the ultimate power of King Phillip II of Spain who commissioned the building of this dramatic granite edifice to demonstrate to the world the dominance of the Spanish crown as well as his Catholic beliefs in defiance of the Protestant Reformation. At a height of 1000m/3280ft, this sombre royal monastery rises up from the foothills of the Sierra de Guadarrama in the northwest of Madrid, approximately 40 km/25 miles from the capital. The four-story complex spans a 161 x 207 m square floor plan with the 90 m/295 ft high dome of the basilica rising in the centre. The façade is covered by 2600 plain, undecorated windows, appearing to hide the vast barracks inside. The architects Juan Bautista de Toledo and Juan de Herrera designed the plans and supervised the pal-

A colossal monastery and palace for the Counter Reformation: El Escorial

SIGHTSEEING

ace's construction (1563–1584) under the watchful eye of the Habsburg king. Only a small section of the entire complex was reserved for the residence of King Philip. El Escorial's main purpose was to serve as a monastery for 100 monks from the Order of Saint Jerome.

Today El Escorial houses a magnificent collection of paintings including works from Tizian, Tintoretto, Peter Paul Rubens, Anthonis van Dyck and Jusepe de Ribera; one outstanding piece is the "The Cavalry" by Rogier van der Weyden. King Philip's bedroom is just one of the royal chambers open to visitors. A steep flight of stairs leads down to the king's pantheon, a windowless room adorned only in red and blue marble where almost all Spain's monarchs from Charles V to Alfonso XIII are interred. It's worth ending the tour by climbing the staircase to the library with its 40,000 precious volumes of books and the basilica opposite.

Tue–Sun 10am–6pm, April–Sept until 8pm | admission 10 euros, Wed/Thu 3 hrs. before closing time free for EU citizens | bus lines 661 and 664 from the underground bus station near the metro stop Moncloa (Metro 3, 6)

ERMITA DE SAN ANTONIO DE LA FLORIDA (126 B–C4) (*C3*)

The tiny chapel has been the burial place of Francisco de Goya since 1919. The chapel's domed ceiling is decorated with one of his frescoes, "The Miracle of St Anthony". *Tue–Sun 9.30am–8pm| free admission | Glorieta San Antonio de la Florida 5 | Metro 6, 10: Príncipe Pío*

MADRID RÍO ★ (126 C 5–6, 130–131 C–F 1–6) (*C–F 4–8*)

Madrid lies on the Manzanares River yet the city's residents have never really appreciated this tributary which is in turn a tributary to the Tagus River. In the 1970s during the Franco dictatorship, an inner ring motorway was built alongside its banks. For several decades the residents simply erased the river from their memories. Yet it has now witnessed a revival. The banks, where traffic once flowed along or, better said, clogged the eight-lane motorway, have been revamped as an enormous greenbelt since 2012. This 120ha green parkland is called Madrid Río, or "Madrid River" and is one of the most astounding feats of modern urban renewal. The construction project resembled at times open heart surgery: while heavy traffic continued along the motorway ring over ground, diggers excavated miles of tunnels in the ground below. Cars now travel underground and the reclaimed ground has been magically transformed into a splendid park along the riverbanks.

On the north end of the park *(Metro 6, 10: Príncipe Pío)*, on the Puente del Rey

(126 C5) (*C–D4*), pedestrians are now treated to panoramic views once reserved for drivers only: the district of Madrid de los Austrias rises up above the Manzanares, with the Royal Palace, cathedral and, further south, the Church of San Francisco el Grande in the background. You are oblivious to the comings and goings underground: engineers successfully interred an entire cross-section of motorway which once crossed over the river.

From Puente del Rey, the Madrid Río stretches 10 km/6 miles along the Manzanares in a south-easterly direction. The river still resembles a stream, just 50 m/164 ft wide and with no risk of drowning (never mind the idea of ships sailing along it). Its murky waters flow quietly along its artificial basalt bed which was constructed to hold the river in the 1940s. The tranquillity and splendid views come to an abrupt halt after 500 m/546 yds of footpath: after passing the Puente de Segovia, Madrid Río transforms into a public park and is occupied by the residents of the dilapidated high-rises on the southwest of the Manzanares. After decades of living next to the motorway, the residents have embraced the park and made it their own as if there had never been anything else standing there other than trees, playgrounds and street cafés. You can find a bicycle tour in the "Discovery Tours" chapter.

PLAZA DE CASTILLA (0) (*0*)

If the "big city" feel of Madrid is eluding you, then head to the Plaza de Castilla at the Paseo de la Castellana in the north of the city, not far from Madrid's northern central train station. Here the American architects, Philip Johnson and John Henry Burgee, built the *Puerta de Europa* in the

On the Plaza de Castilla, Madrid acts (post)modern with the Puerta de Europa

Whether in flesh, blood or bronze: *matadores* are Madrid's gladiators

1990s as a modern-day city gate: two towers that lean towards one another at a 15 degree angle. Most people refer to the steel and aluminium clad black glass towers after its original owners, the Kuwait Investment Office, *Torres KIO.* At "only" 107 m/351 ft tall and with 27 storeys the towers hardly qualify as real skyscrapers, but their unusual shape has definitely made them Madrid's unofficial landmark. The dazzling gold stele in the centre of the square, the 92 m/301 ft high *Obelisco de Calatrava,* was designed by the Valencian architect Santiago Calatrava. One and a half kilometres (1 mile) to the north stand four gigantic skyscrapers towering over Madrid's skyline, the *Cuatro Torres,* including Spain's highest building (250 m/820 ft), the *Torre Foster* designed by the Brit Norman Foster. The towers are not open to the public. They house offices, banks and the luxury hotel *Eurostars Madrid Tower Hotel (474 rooms | tel. 9 13 34 27 00 |* *www.eurostarsmadridtower.com | Expensive). Metro 1, 9, 10: Plaza Castilla*

PLAZA DE TOROS LAS VENTAS
(0) (*m L2*)

Even if bullfights are not your thing, you will nevertheless be impressed by this monumental arena at the intersection of Calle de Alcalá and the city motorway east of the Salamanca district. It was built in the mock Mudejar style with hundreds of Moorish horseshoe arches characterising its brick façade. The first *corrida* took place here in 1934 and the massive arena seats 24,000, making it the third largest bullfighting arena in the world. Today it is not only used for bullfights but also for open air concerts hosted by both local and international performers. *Tours with audioguide daily 10am–5.30pm (until 1 pm on corrida days) | admission 12 euros | C/ de Alcalá 237 | lasventastour.com | Metro 2, 5: Ventas*

FOOD & DRINK

The Spanish love their food. When they start talking about what makes their country special, its cuisine always ranks on top of the list.

It is no doubt that Spanish cuisine relies on using excellent ingredients: fresh vegetables, fresh meat and above all fresh fish and seafood. On the outskirts of Madrid the world's second-largest fish market only for wholesalers (Tokyo's is the largest) opens its doors every morning. Fish, cold pressed olive oil, legumes and a glass of red wine are the basics of the Mediterranean diet.

Aside from olive oil, salt and pepper, and some garlic, the Castilians traditionally tend to add very little else to their dishes. It is precisely this that they love about their cooking, the fact that the pure taste of the top quality tomatoes, or sea bass, or pork or mussels is allowed to shine through. Sophisticated sauces, spices or combinations of vegetable are not the style of Spanish cuisine. A steak quickly grilled with a little oil served with homemade potato chips – and there you have your classic Madrid main course.

The cooking traditions along the coast tend to be richer and more varied than those inland. Of course you can savour all these dishes in Madrid as well and it goes without saying that you will find excellent fine dining restaurants in the Spanish capital. If you order a simple lunch menu for around 10 euros you can expect a good meal, although not necessarily a work of art.

Fresh, top quality ingredients and simple recipes – these are the secrets of the delicious and unpretentious Castilian cuisine

Spanish mealtimes can take a little getting used to for tourists. In the evenings restaurants usually only open at around 9pm and on a weekend it is not unusual to meet for dinner much later, say at 11pm. Lunch is typically served between 2pm and 4pm.

CAFÉS

CAFÉ COMERCIAL (128 A3) (*ꝏ F2*)
A revolving door takes you into the entrance area with its tapas bar, behind it is a café –Madrid's oldest – with leather seats and marble tables. An institution in Madrid that has been around since 1887. *Mon–Sat 7.30am–1am, Sun 9am–midnight | Glorieta de Bilbao 7 | Metro 1, 4: Bilbao*

CAFÉ DEL NUNCIO (122 B4) (*ꝏ E5*)
A classic interior with a INSIDERTIP relaxed outdoor café on the steps of the Costanilla del Nuncio in the heart of La Latina. *Daily 12.30pm–2.30am | C/ Segovia 9 | Metro 5: La Latina*

CAFÉ GIJÓN ● (128 B5) (*G4*)

Madrid's most famous café. Since 1888, the literary types meet up here, from Ramón de la Valle-Inclán to Arturo Pérez-Reverte. *Daily 7.30am–1.30am | Paseo de Recoletos 21 | Metro 4: Colón*

EL ESPEJO ★ (128 C4) (*G3*)

This café is in a glass conservatory in the middle of the Paseo de Recoletos pedestrian boulevard and has been around since 1978. The interior is done out in a beautiful art nouveau style. *Daily 9am–1am | Paseo de Recoletos 31 | Metro 4: Colón*

NUEVO CAFÉ BARBIERI (123 D5) (*F6*)

This café has the feel of a Viennese coffee shop with its iron columns and marble-topped tables. It may not be as upmarket as it once was but that is the special charm of the Barbieri. *Daily 4pm–2am | C/ Ave María 45 | Metro 3: Lavapiés*

INSIDER TIP OITA CAFÉ ☻ (123 D1) (*F3*)

Exquisite homemade pastries served with organic tea or coffee with normal milk or soya milk. *Mon–Thu 9am–10pm, Fri/Sat 9am–2am, Sun 10am–10pm | C/ Hortaleza 30 | Metro 1, 5: Gran Vía*

DINING ALFRESCO

CASA DE GRANADA 🍃 (122 C4) (*F5*)

Andalusian tapas bar with splendid view from its balcony on the 6th floor. Ring the bell downstairs to enter the building! *Daily | C/ Doctor Cortezo 17 | tel. 91 36 93 596 | Metro 1: Tirso de Molina | Budget*

IROCO (129 D4) (*H3*)

Elegant restaurant in the Salamanca *barrio* that serves international cuisine, also with the option of a table on the garden terrace. *Daily | C/ de Velázquez 18 | tel. 914 31 73 81 | Metro 4: Velázquez | Moderate–Expensive*

The Plaza Olavide transforms into one large outdoor restaurant on fine days

LA TITA RIVERA (123 D1) (*ⅲ F3*)
Casual courtyard restaurant attracting a young crowd which serves homemade hamburgers or burritos to accompany a beer. *Daily | C/ Pérez Galdós 4 | tel. 9 15 22 18 90 | Metro 1, 5: Gran Vía | Budget*

INSIDER TIP **PLAZA OLAVIDE**
(128 A2) (*ⅲ F2*)
The round, tree lined square in Chamberí is a veritable beehive on a fine day. The dozens of outdoor tables of the eight simple restaurants all get snapped up quickly. A popular lunchtime option is *tortilla de patatas* and a big bowl of salad to share. *Metro 1, 2: Iglesia, Quevedo | Budget*

TAQUERÍA DEL ALAMILLO
(122 A4) (*ⅲ E5*)
This place only has a few coveted tables tucked away amid plenty of potted plants. It is in a charming building in the historic Madrid de los Austrias and serves traditional Mexican cuisine. *Closed Tue lunchtime and Mon | Plaza del Alamillo 8 | tel. 913 64 20 88 | Metro 5: La Latina | Moderate*

RESTAURANTS: EXPENSIVE

ALABASTER (128 C6) (*ⅲ H4*)
The Galician owners of this restaurant (close to the Plaza de Cibeles) cannot disguise their Atlantic roots: fish and seafood are the highlights. Contemporary simple cuisine made from first-class ingredients and served in an elegant yet relaxing setting. *Closed Sun | C/ de Montalbán 9 | tel. 9 15 12 11 31 | www.restaurantealabaster.com | Metro 2: Banco de España*

INSIDER TIP **LA FAVORITA**
(128 A3) (*ⅲ F2*)
Serving creative cuisine in a congenial atmosphere, this restaurant also has a small section with five tables in a walled garden. But the waiters are the real reason

you should visit – they are all professional singers who ensure that you have an operatic accompaniment to your meal. Madrid has two other opera-style restaurants but true to its name La Favorita remains the favourite. *Closed Sun, closed Sat lunchtime | C/ Covarrubias 25 | tel. 914 48 38 10 | www.restaurantelafavorita.com | Metro 1, 4, 5, 10: Alonso Martínez, Iglesia*

JULIÁN DE TOLOSA
(122 B4) (*ⅲ E5*)
One of the classics on the Cava Baja, Madrid's restaurant mile. It is renowned for

---

★ **El Espejo**
Madrid's charming place to enjoy a cup of coffee → p. 58

★ **DiverXO**
Madrid's only three-starred restaurant – with an edgy and outlandish chef → p. 60

★ **La Tasquita de Enfrente**
Eat in style in the historic Malasaña district → p. 60

★ **Platea Madrid**
Star-rated food in a former cinema: pleasure for the palate and eyes → p. 60

★ **Matritum**
Fine tapas and elaborate main courses → p. 61

★ **Casa Mingo**
Chicken and *sidra* – the Asturias in Madrid → p. 63

★ **Almendro 13**
Authentic tapas in a traditional district → p. 65

MARCO POLO HIGHLIGHTS

its Basque meat dishes. Try the *chuletón,* the excellent (and enormous) steak! *Closed Sun evening | C/ Cava Baja 18 | tel. 913 65 82 10 | juliandetolosa.com | Metro 5: La Latina*

LA TASQUITA DE ENFRENTE ★
(123 D1) (*ⓜ F4*)
The location of this tiny taverna, in a folksy corner of Malasaña, has not prevented gourmets from flocking to it. Creative Spanish cuisine, everything fresh from the market. *Closed Sun | C/ Ballesta 6 | tel. 915 32 54 49 | www.latasquitadeen frente.com | Metro 1, 3, 5: Gran Vía, Callao*

PLATEA MADRID ★ (128 C4) (*ⓜ H3*)
Superlatives spring to mind when talking about this culinary treasure. In 2014 this former cinema was artfully transformed into a gourmet theatre, covering 6000m^2 over four floors. Almost everyone who's anyone on Madrid's culinary scene is based here. Housing half a dozen tapas bars, a confectionery, a cocktail bar – it also offers guests the chance to get to know the chefs Paco Roncero or Ramón Freixa (his Arriba restaurant on the first floor offers the best views) at modest prices. *Daily | C/ de Goya 5 | www.plateama drid.com | Metro 4: Colón, Serrano*

RESTAURANTS: MODERATE

BOLÍVAR (127 F3) (*ⓜ F2*)
Mediterranean cuisine fresh from the market right in the heart of the historic

GOURMET RESTAURANTS

DiverXO ★ (125 D2) (*ⓜ O*)
David Muñoz (born 1980) is the enfant terrible among Spanish chefs labelled as exciting, edgy and bold. One critic once described his restaurant in the Hotel NH Eurobuilding as being the "cirque du soleil" on the gastronomic scene. Poetry for the palate and a spectacle for all senses. *145–200 euros | closed Sun/Mon | C/ Padre Damián 23 | tel. 915 70 07 66 | www.diverxo.com | Metro 10: Cuzco*

Ramón Freixa Madrid (128 C3) (*ⓜ H2*)
The Catalan chef Ramón Freixa at Hotel Único wants his food to be "entertaining and fun", as well as innovative and edgy – although some diners are put off by too much experimenting, most rave about the experience. *Menu 85–135 euros | closed Sun/Mon | C/ de Claudio Coello 67 | tel. 917 81 82 62 | www.ramon freixamadrid.com | Metro 4: Serrano*

Santceloni (128 C1) (*ⓜ H1*)
The classic among Madrid's luxury restaurants. Housed in Hotel Hesperia, chef Óscar Velasco offers guests the finest home-style cooking accompanied by delicious aromas from the restaurant's cheese table. *From 150 euros | closed Sun, closed Sat lunchtime | Paseo de la Castellana 57 | tel. 912 10 88 40 | www. restaurantesantceloni.com | Metro 7, 10: Gregorio Marañón*

Sergi Arola (128 B2) (*ⓜ G2*)
One of the most creative minds on the Spanish culinary circuit. A pupil of Ferran Adrià and Pierre Gagnaire, the Catalan Sergi Arola claims to have "rediscovered the magic of cooking" with this restaurant. *Lunch menu 49, degustation menu 135 euros | Closed Sun/Mon | C/ Zurbano 31 | tel. 913 10 21 69 | www.sergiarola.es | Metro 5: Rubén Darío*

Rustic elegance in the unpretentious Malasaña: La Tasquita de Enfrente

Malasaña district. Try the pork loin in an aromatic port wine reduction or the *chipirones*, baby squid. *Closed Sun | C/ Manuela Malasaña 28 | tel. 914 45 12 74 | www.restaurantebolivar.com | Metro 1, 4: Bilbao*

INSIDER TIP CON DOS FOGONES
(127 E4) (*Ø E3*)

This colourful and cosy restaurant serves unpretentious international cuisine. Popular with the younger crowd. *Daily | C/ San Bernardino 9 | tel. 915 59 63 26 | www.condosfogones.com | Metro 3, 10: Plaza de España*

GOURMET EXPERIENCE GRAN VÍA ⚡
(122 C2) (*Ø E–F4*)

You haven't seen Madrid if you haven't visited the 9th floor of the Corte Inglés at the Plaza Callao. The restaurant has ten self-service counters offering a range of tasty foods from traditional Spanish to Asian to be enjoyed with the INSIDER TIP breathtaking view over the Gran Vía. *Daily | Plaza de Callao 2 | Metro 3, 5 : Callao*

LA BIOTIKA (123 E4) (*Ø F5*)

Madrid's oldest vegetarian restaurant, serving macrobiotic and vegan cooking. Cosy and down-to-earth decorations. With a 🌀 store selling organic food. *Daily | C/ Amor de Dios 3 | tel. 9 14 29 07 80 | www.labiotika.es | Metro 1: Antón Martín*

LA COCINA DE SAN ANTÓN ⚡
(123 E1) (*Ø G3*)

The indoor market hall in Chueca is a popular meeting place for diners. This restaurant serves traditional Spanish cuisine on its *azotea* – rooftop terrace – with views over the district's streets. Ideal spot to taste freshly cut *Bellota* ham with a glass of red wine *Daily | Mercado de San Antón | C/ Augusto Figueroa 24 | tel. 9 13 30 02 94 | www.lacocinadesananton.com | Metro 5: Chueca*

MATRITUM ⭐ (122 B4) (*Ø E5*)

Not very spacious, usually packed and often noisy, yet this restaurant still manages to retain its elegance. A great selec-

LOCAL SPECIALITIES

albóndigas – meatballs
boquerones fritos/en vinagre – deep fried/marinated anchovies
café solo/cortado/con leche – espresso/espresso with a shot of milk/milk coffee
calamares – squid
callos madrileños – tripe stew
caña – a small glass of beer
cava – Spanish sparkling wine
chipirones – baby squid
chorizo – paprika salami (photo left)
churros – deep fried pastry, particularly popular *con chocolate* i.e. dunked in hot chocolate (photo right)
clara – beer shandy/ beer with *gaseosa* (carbonated lemonade)
cochinillo – suckling pig
cocido madrileño – typical Madrid stew with *chorizo, garbanzos* (chickpeas) and vegetables
cordero (asado) – (roast) lamb

croquetas – fish, meat or ham croquettes
ensaladilla – potato salad with greens (fresh or cooked) and mayonnaise (plenty of it)
gambas al ajillo/a la plancha – prawns in garlic sauce/grilled on a hot metal plate
horchata – refreshingly sweet drink made from ground tiger nuts
jamón – air dried ham
mejillones – mussels
pulpo – octopus
patatas bravas – fried potatoes served in a spicy tomato sauce
pollo – chicken
queso – farmhouse cheese, mostly *Manchego* (from La Mancha)
tinto de verano – "summer wine", a mix of half wine and half *gaseosa* with plenty of ice
tortilla – Spanish potato omelette

---

tion of unusual tapas (Catalan and international) with an extensive wine list. *Closed Mon, closed Tue lunchtime | C/ Cava Alta 17 | tel. 913 65 82 37 | www.tabernamatritum.es | Metro 5: La Latina*

MERCADO DE LA REINA
(123 E2) (*ɯ F4*)
A restaurant in a Mediterranean market setting furnished with long bars, long tables, an olive tree next to the entrance and a lively crowd of young people enjoying life and Spanish cuisine.

Daily | Gran Vía 12 | tel. 9 15 21 31 98 | www.mercadodelareina.es | Metro 1, 5: Gran Vía

INSIDER TIP **RIBEIRA DO MIÑO**
(126 A4) *(ᗞ F3)*

This popular Galician restaurant is usually packed to the hilt and is famous for its seafood. If you order a *mariscada* then you get to have a taste of everything – a generous platter of Atlantic seafood that is a real treat. *Closed Mon | C/ Santa Brígida 1 | tel. 915 21 98 54 | www.marisqueriaribeiradomino.com | Metro 1, 10: Tribunal*

TIRADITO (127 E3) *(ᗞ E2)*

Master chef Omar Malpartida reinterprets Peruvian cuisine with his warm *ceviche* for example (raw fish marinated in lime juice which is normally served cold). A real gem! *Closed Mon, closed Tue evenings | C/ Conde Duque 13 | tel. 9 15 41 78 76 | tiradito.es | Metro 2, 4: San Bernardo*

RESTAURANTS: BUDGET

BAZAAR
(123 E1) *(ᗞ G4)*

This young, hip restaurant in the Chueca district has a cool colonial-style interior and is recommended for its delicious international cuisine. *Daily | C/ de la Libertad 21 | no reservations | www.restaurantbazaar.com | Metro 5: Chueca*

CASA MINGO ★
(126 C4) *(ᗞ C3)*

A classic since 1888, although there's (almost) only roast chicken, salad and *sidra* on offer. On a fine day rows of tables are crammed on to the street. *Daily | Paseo de la Florida 34 | no reservations | Metro 6, 10: Príncipe Pío*

INSIDER TIP **EL ESTRAGÓN VEGETARIANO** (122 B4) *(ᗞ E5)*

Unpretentious vegetarian restaurant in a picturesque corner of the La Latina district. *Daily | Plaza de la Paja 10 | tel. 9 13 65 89 82 | www.elestragonvegetariano.com | Metro 5: La Latina*

EN BUSCA DEL TIEMPO
(123 D3) *(ᗞ F5)*

Delicious Basque-Catalan country cooking with some dishes cooked directly on the BBQ. Its specialty is toasted bread with grilled pork loins or mushrooms and Basque cheese. *Daily | C/ Barcelona 4 | tel. 9 15 21 98 01 | www.restauranteeltiempo.com | Metro 1, 2, 3 :Sol*

LA MUSA LATINA (122 B4) *(ᗞ E5)*

The coolest bar and restaurant on the Plaza de la Paja, the prettiest square in La Latina. Creative international cuisine accompanied by DJ music. *Daily | Costan-*

LOW BUDGET

On a budget but you want to be sure to get at least one full meal a day? Lunchtime, not nighttime, is when most restaurants offer a full three-course affordable set menu from Monday to Friday.

Museo del Jamón (www.museodeljamon.com) is a chain of stores specialising in Spanish hams. Decorated with huge legs of cured ham hanging from the ceiling, simple *bocadillos* and tapas are served at the bar at moderate prices. Try the branch in the *Carrera de San Jerónimo 6* **(123 D3)** *(ᗞ F4)* *(Metro 1, 2, 3: Sol)*.

illa de San Andrés 12 | tel. 9 13 54 02 55 | www.grupolamusa.com | Metro 5: La Latina

PUBLIC (127 F5) (*m F4*)

That's what it's like on the other side of the Gran Vía: Where in the streets bored

SHAPLA (132 A2) (*m F6*)

The Lavapiés *barrio* and Indian food go hand in hand and the Shapla's deliciously spicy cuisine makes it a favourite amongst Madrid's locals so you can consider yourself lucky if you can find a table beneath the trees. *Daily | C/ Lavapiés 42 | tel.*

Traditional Madrid: tapas bars adorned with tiles such as La Chata along the Cava Baja

prostitutes linger, an interesting culinary treat awaits next door. At the Public , you can get good interantional fare at affordable prices. Because there are large crowds quite frequently, the service might become a bit hectic at times. *Daily | Desengaño 11 | no reservations | www.restaurantpublic.com | Metro 3, 5: Callao*

915 28 15 99 | www.shaplaindianrestaurant.com | Metro 3: Lavapiés

TAPAS

Trekking through Madrid *de tapas* means keeping your calm and not being deterred by the crowds in front of the counter and all thee occupied tables. Usually tapas bars don't accept reservations but don't worry, sooner or later you will be served. Tapas on their own are usually small portions and one portion is not really a meal. Larger portions are called *raciones*.

ALMENDRO 13 ⭐ (122 B4) (*ṁ E5*)

A classic serving traditional rustic Spanish cuisine. You place your order at the hatch and a bell rings when the food is ready. The shop is often so packed that patrons are left sitting on their car bonnets outside waiting for their order. *Daily | C/ Almendro 13 | Metro 5: La Latina*

AUTOMÁTICO (123 E5) (*ṁ F6*)

The most popular (tapas) bar in the Lavapiés district, with tables outside in summer. A magazine survey voted its *ensaladilla rusa*, a tapas classic, as the best in Madrid. *Closed Mon–Thu lunchtime | C/ Argumosa 17 | Metro 3: Lavapiés*

INSIDER TIP ▶ BAR AMOR
(127 F3) (*ṁ F2*)

Rustic stone walls and flowers are not usually part of the design in Malasaña. Excellent tapas available at the bar or in the restaurant area. It's hard to find a table in the evening. *Closed Sun/Mon | C/ de Manuela Malasaña 22 | tel. 915944829 | Metro 1, 4: Bilbao*

BOCAÍTO (123 E1) (*ṁ G4*)

The small room in front of the counter is usually packed because the traditional (Castilian and Andalusian) tapas served here are excellent. Not on the cheap side. *Closed Sun | C/ Libertad 6 | Metro 2, 5: Chueca, Banco de España*

CASA LABRA (127 F6) (*ṁ F4*)

Tapas bar oozing with typical Madrid charm. Croquetas and bacalao are served at the entrance to be eaten with a drink ordered at the bar. Spain's socialist party was founded here in 1879. *Daily | C/ de*

Tetuán 12 | tel. 915310081 | www. casalabra.es | Metro 1, 2, 3: Sol

CAVA BAJA ● (122 B4) (*ṁ E5*)

The entire Calle Cava Baja is lined with traditional restaurants and tapas bars. Creative tapas are served at *Casa Lucas* (no. 30). Great alternatives: *La Taberna del Tempranillo (no. 38)*, *Taberna Txakolina (no. 26)*, *Esteban (no. 36)*, *La Chata (no. 24)* and *La Antoñita (no. 14)*. *Metro 5: La Latina*

CERVECERÍA CERVANTES
(123 E3) (*ṁ G5*)

Traditional tapas bar in the lower part of Huerta. Not the cheapest but the octopus galician style and the *gambas* are delicious. *Closed Sun evenings | Plaza de Jesús 7 | Metro 1, 2: Banco de España, Antón Martín*

JUANA LA LOCA (122 B4) (*ṁ E5*)

A must on your tapas crawl through La Latina. A wide variety of *pinchos* (kebabs) and tapas. *Closed Mon lunchtime | Plaza Puerta de Moros 4 | Metro 5: La Latina*

INSIDER TIP ▶ LA MONTERÍA
(129 E5) (*ṁ J4*)

Restaurant with one of the best selection of tapas located directly behind the Retiro park. *Tigres* (stuffed mussels) are the specialty of the house. *Closed Sun evenings. | C/ de Lope de Rueda 35 | Metro 9: Ibiza*

LA VENENCIA (132 A1) (*ṁ F5*)

Try a chilled Manzanilla sherry which is perfect with the *mojama* (air dried tuna). Despite the influx of tourists, the restaurant has been able to retain its authenticity. *Closed lunchtime | C/ Echegaray 7 | Metro 2: Sevilla*

SHOPPING

Yes, it is quite true that clothes and shoes are still a little cheaper in Madrid than elsewhere in Europe. But be weary – many local and international designer boutiques are not shy to charge you big city prices, noble boutiques sell little fabric for many euros. Still, shopping in Madrid is great fun!

If you want to save money and browsing through the second-hand items on offer at the Sunday Rastro is not quite your thing, then look out for the *rebajas* (sales) instead: they are seasonal from January to March and in July/August. Traditional stores open their doors from Monday to Friday between 10am and 2pm and again from 5pm to 8pm, as well as on a Saturday morning. However, most shops in the big shopping streets

Shoppers' paradise Madrid – bargain hunt at the flea markets or shop in style on the Calle de Fuencarral

skip the long midday break and are also open on Saturday afternoons and Sundays – Madrid has very liberal shop closing laws.

The main shopping streets in the city centre are *Calle de Preciados* and the *Calle Carmen* between Puerta del Sol and Plaza Callao. It may be a pedestrian zone lacking in charm but it makes up for it by having a vast array of fashion and everyday items offered at decent prices. North of it is the *Gran Vía* between Plaza España and Red de San Luis. Despite the heavy

traffic this has become a busy shopping area.

The *barrios* of Malasaña and Chueca are at the heart of young fashion with the ★ *Calle de Fuencarral* running between them. Once a run down street, for a while it was the city's hippest area – a little bit of London in Madrid. For creative designers or shop owners who don't have the financial backing of big conglomerates, the rents in the Calle Fuencarral have become prohibitively expensive so they have turned instead to the side streets, e.g. the INSIDER TIP *Calle Espíritu Santo.* North of the old town, there's the ★ *Calle de Serrano* in the elegant Salamanca barrio with its wide sidewalks, an ideal area for some pleasant high-end shopping.

Browse through four floors of the French multimedia store FNAC

BOOKS & MULTIMEDIA

DESNIVEL (123 D4) *(∅ F5)*
This shop i is a must if you want to go cycling or hiking in the nearby Sierra de Guadarrama: well informed staff to assist you with maps and mountain climbing books. *Plaza Matute 6 | Metro 1: Antón Martín*

EL FLAMENCO VIVE ★
(122 B3) *(∅ E4)*
The store has the widest selection of flamenco CDs, literature, guitars and costumes. You can also browse and order online at *www.elflamencovive.com. C/ Conde de Lemos 7 | Metro 2, 5: Ópera*

FNAC (122 C2) *(∅ F4)*
This French multimedia chain store offers a great selection of books, CDs, computer and photography accessories on four floors. *C/ Preciados 28 | www.fnac.es | Metro 3, 5: Callao*

LA CENTRAL (122 C2) *(∅ E4)*
Madrid's paradise for book worms: 70,000 books on 1200 m² stretched over 3 floors. Café restaurant and cocktail bar. *C/ del Postigo de San Martín 8 | www.la central.com | Metro 3, 5: Callao*

LA LIBRERÍA (122 A3) *(∅ E5)*
Specialising in Madrid literature since 1986. *C/ Mayor 80 | www.edicioneslalibreria. com | Metro 2, 5: Ópera*

DELICATESSEN

ANTIGUA PASTELERÍA DEL POZO (123 D3) *(∅ F4)*
Founded in 1830, this is Madrid's oldest bakery. *C/ Pozo 8 | Metro 1, 2, 3: Sol*

CACAO SAMPACA (128 B4) *(∅ G3)*
A feast of the senses for chocoholics: the best homemade specialities to take away or try right there. *C/ Orellana 4 | www. cacaosampaka.com | Metro 4, 5, 10: Alonso Martínez*

CASA MIRA (123 E3) *(∅ F4)*
Specialising in marzipan, this is also where locals buy their special Christmas nougat or *turrón. Carrera San Jerónimo 30 | Metro 2: Sevilla*

EL HUERTO DE LUCAS ⊚
(128 B4) *(∅ G3)*
An organic store, market and restaurant rolled into one: Madrid's best selection

of organic food is available here in Chueca. *C/ San Lucas 13 | elhuertodelucas. com | Metro 5: Chueca*

INSIDER TIP EL JARDÍN DEL CONVENTO
(122 B3) *(Ø E5)*
Jams, honey and other sweet delights produced in Spanish monasteries are the kind of specialities you will find at this quaint shop on the Plaza de la Villa. *C/ del Cordón 1 | Metro 2, 5: Ópera*

GÓNDIAZ (122 A1) *(Ø E4)*
In this small shop near the Royal Palace, some of the best hams in Spain are bathed in subdued lighting and hang suspended from the ceiling. *Plaza Marina Española 7 | www.gondiaz.es | Metro 2: Santo Domingo*

LAVINIA (129 D3) *(Ø H2)*
A world of wines! Around 4500 labels (both local and international) in addition to *cavas,* brandy and some rare and unusual spirits. You can grab a bite to eat at the gourmet club and enjoy a bottle of wine with your meal at shop floor prices. *C/ de José Ortega y Gasset 16 | www.lavinia.es | Metro 5, 9: Núñez de Balboa*

PATRIMONIO COMUNAL OLIVARERO ⊙ (128 A4) *(Ø G3)*
Around 150 different *virgen extra* – the finest olive oil quality you can buy – adorn the shelves of this small and simple store. Orders also online at *www.pco.es. C/ de Mejía Lequerica 1 | Metro 4, 5, 10: Alonso Martínez*

INSIDER TIP QUESERÍA CONDE DUQUE ⊙ (127 E3) *(Ø E2)*
Rounds upon rounds of cheese supplied every week by artisan Spanish cheesemakers are stacked on the shop's shelves. A splendid, mouth-watering sight! *C/*

Conde Duque 15 | queseriacondeduque. com | Metro 2, 4: San Bernardo

FLEA MARKET

RASTRO ★ ● (122 C5) *(Ø E5–6)*
On a Sunday morning you will always find the streets surrounding the Plaza Cascorro full of people. For Madrileños spending time at the Rastro is as much a part of their Sunday routine as attending mass is. Some 80,000 people visit more than 1300 stalls. If you want to discover unusual items, you should turn up at 9am already. For many the flea market is simply a good excuse to meet up with friends afterwards to enjoy some wine and tapas at one of the many bars in the area. From the Plaza Cascorro head down the Ribera

MARCO POLO HIGHLIGHTS

★ **El Flamenco Vive**
Spanish flamenco heaven → p. 68

★ **Rastro**
Madrid's exuberant flea market → p. 69

★ **Casa de Diego**
Fanning like the Spanish → p. 73

★ **Mercado de San Miguel**
Beautiful market in Madrid's historic old town → p. 71

★ **Calle de Fuencarral**
Madrid's coolest shopping street → p. 67

★ **Calle de Serrano**
A fashion designer behind every door → p. 68

de Curtidores which has lots of little side streets where you can find anything. Bargain to your heart's content but always keep your eyes peeled for pickpockets! *Metro 1, 5: Tirso de Molina, La Latina, Puerta de Toledo*

DEPARTMENT STORES/ SHOPPING CENTRES

If you are looking for something specific and don't know where to start your best bet is *Corte Inglés*, a chain of department stores and a Spanish institution. There are two inner city outlets: (122 C2) (*∅ F4*)

(C/ Preciados 3 | Metro 1, 2, 3: Sol; Plaza de Callao 1 | Metro 3, 5: Callao.
The most attractive shopping centres in town are the *ABC Serrano* ((128 C3) (*∅ H2*) | *C/ de Serrano 61 | Metro 5: Rubén Darío*) with around 80 shops and the ● *Centro Comercial Príncipe Pío* (126 C5) (*∅ D4*) (*Metro 6, 10: Príncipe Pío*) at the eponymous train station below the Royal Palace with around 100 shops, restaurants and cinemas.

LOW BUDGET

Do you like Camper shoes? This Spanish shoe brand is cheaper here than elsewhere in Europe. You can find them here: *Gran Vía 54* **(122 C1)** **(*∅ E4*)** *Metro 3, 5: Callao; C/ de Fuencarral 42* **(128 A4)** **(*∅ F3*)** *Metro 1, 5: Gran Vía; C/ de Serrano 24* **(128 C4)** **(*∅ H3*)** *Metro 4: Serrano*

Las Rozas Village **(0)** **(*∅ 0*)** attracts shoppers with 100 brand-name boutiques. There is a bus connection from the Plaza de España to the outlet centre in the north of the city. More information available at *www. lasrozasvillage.com/shoppingexpress*

Madrid's largest ● *producer market (mercadoproductores.es)* specialising in organic food is held on the last weekend of every month *(Sat 11am–7pm, Sun 11am–5pm)* at the *Matadero Madrid cultural centre* **(132 A6)** **(*∅ F8*)** *(Paseo de la Chopera 14 | Metro 3, 6: Legazpi)*

ART GALLERIES

LA FÁBRICA (123 F4) (*∅ G5*)
Exhibition space and cultural centre with café, library and studios behind the Caixa Forum. Specialises in photography. *C/ Alameda 9 | lafabrica.com | Metro 1: Atocha*

GALERÍA JUANA DE AIZPURU
(128 B4) (*∅ G3*)
Juana de Aizpuru was the mastermind behind and first director of Madrid's art exhibition, Arco. She is still one of the most influential figures on the Spanish art scene. She promotes promising con-

In the Príncipe Pío station, you can boost the economy at the Centro Comercial

temporary artists in her gallery. *C/ Barquillo 44 | juanadeaizpuru.es | Metro 5: Chueca*

MADRID DF (123 E5–6) (*Ⓜ G6*)

DF stands for Doctor Fourquet, the name of the small street in Lavapiés behind the Reina Sofía museum where the influential gallery owner Helga de Alvear opened her first gallery in 1995. Another 13 galleries have followed – no other city in Europe can probably boast more galleries per square mile. To encourage more visitors inside the galleries, the Agenda Magenta platform organises guided tours on Tuesdays and Thursdays at 5.30pm and Saturdays at 12.30pm for 8 euros. More details can be found at *visitasdf.com. C/ del Doctor Fourquet 12 | Metro 1: Atocha*

INDOOR MARKETS

The capital is home to 48 indoor market halls where many of Madrid's locals do their daily shopping. Few of the market halls carry any architectural importance but they are all full of the fresh smells of fish, chicken, sausage, cheese, fruit and vegetables. If you want to soak up the atmosphere of one of these popular market halls, head out in the morning to the *Mercado de Antón Martín* (123 E4) (*Ⓜ F5*) (*C/ de Santa Isabel 5 | Metro 1: Antón Martín*) or the *Mercado de los Mostenses* (127 E4) (*Ⓜ E3*) (*Plaza de los Mostenses 1 | Metro 3, 10: Plaza de España*).

MERCADO DE SAN MIGUEL ★
(122 B3) (*Ⓜ E4–5*)

The city's most beautiful market hall is not a traditional market anymore but has become a privately run haven for gourmets. Today the glass-and-steel structure next to the Plaza Mayor that dates back to 1916 is home to well-stocked fruit, cheese and fish stalls, a sherry bar and café that has delicious pastries and a stall selling Ⓥ *bacalao* (salted cod) from sustainable fish farms. *Sun–Wed 10am–midnight, Thu–Sat 10am–2am | Plaza de San Miguel | www.mercadodesanmiguel. es |Metro 2, 5: Ópera*

FASHION, SHOES & ACCESSORIES

AGATHA RUIZ DE LA PRADA
(128 C4) (*W H3*)
Madrid's most famous fashion designer likes rich bold colours and designs, there is also a children's collection. *C/ de Serrano 27 | www.agatharuizdelaprada.com | Metro 4: Serrano*

Fuencarral 29 | www.custo.com| Metro 5: Chueca

KLING (123 D1) (*W F4*)
Madrid's fashion label for young women – it stands for bold, edgy, girly and retro.
Also sells shoes and accessories. *C/ de la Ballesta 4 | www.kling.es | Metro 3, 5: Callao*

Flamenco, pop or classical music – Ramírez guitars have a national reputation

CALIGAE (123 E1) (*W G3*)
The Calle Augusto Figueroa in the Chueca district is Madrid's shoe heaven. This unassuming store sells rows on rows of shoes from the most exciting Spanish designers such as Chie Mihara. *C/ Augusto Figueroa 31 | Metro 5: Chueca*

CUSTO (128 A4) (*W F3*)
Barcelona's top fashion designers' creations are glamorous and colourful and are far cheaper here than abroad. *C/ de*

LOEWE (128 C4) (*W H3*)
Elegant, classic and very pricey. They sell the most exclusive Spanish handbags and leather goods. *C/ de Serrano 26 and 34 | www.loewe.com |Metro 4: Serrano*

INSIDER TIP ▶ OJALÁ (123 D3) (*W F5*)
Paloma del Pozo has made her name as one of the most creative names on the Spanish fashion scene – classic cuts, exquisite fabrics and daring yet elegant patterns. Prices are at the high end of the

price range. *C/ de las Huertas 5 | www.ojala.es | Metro 1: Antón Martín*

EL TEMPLO DE SUSO (127 F4) (*Ⓜ F3*)
Vintage is in fashion in Malasaña and this tiny store was one of the first to start selling second-hand clothing. *C/ del Espíritu Santo 1 | Metro 1, 10: Tribunal*

INSIDER TIP ▸ TRAKABARRAKA
(127 F4) (*Ⓜ E3*)
Young, vibrant fashion from Bilbao inspired by the elegance of decades gone by sold in a small boutique in Malasaña. *C/ del Pez 36 | trakabarraka.com | Metro 2: Noviciado*

SOUVENIRS, ARTS & CRAFTS UNIQUE TO SPAIN

ANTIGUA CASA TALAVERA
(122 B1) (*Ⓜ E4*)
Since 1904, exclusive handmade items by the leaders in Spanish ceramics like Talavera de la Reina or Granada. *C/ Isabel la Católica 2 | Metro 2: Santo Domingo*

CASA DE DIEGO ★
(123 D2) (*Ⓜ F4*)
Mañana lloverá says the sign at the entrance, which means "rain is forecast for tomorrow". Casa de Diego has been selling umbrellas and walking sticks since 1858, as well as their own line of handheld fans. *Puerta del Sol 12 | www.casadediego.net |Metro 1, 2, 3: Sol*

CASA JIMÉNEZ (122 C2) (*Ⓜ F4*)
This is where tradition conscious Madrileños buy their *mantones* (fringed shawls) and *mantillas* (lace veils also covering the head). *C/ Preciados 42 | Metro 3, 5: Callao*

JOSÉ RAMÍREZ (122 C3) (*Ⓜ F5*)
Guitar manufacturer José Ramírez established his workshop at the end of the 19th century. Today it is run by his great-grand-daughter, Amalia Ramírez. Spain's best guitar players buy their instruments here. *C/ de la Paz 8 | www.guitarrasramirez.com | Metro 1, 2, 3: Sol*

MADRID[3]
(123 D3) (*Ⓜ F5*)
A store selling unusual souvenirs of Madrid. Also a popular haunt of locals. *C/ de la Cruz 35 | www.madridalcubo.com | Metro 1, 2, 3: Sol*

SESEÑA (123 D3) (*Ⓜ F4*)
Capas (capes) is a classical Spanish item of clothing i.e. sleeveless coat worn by both men and women. They sell only top quality items. *C/ Cruz 23 | www.sesena.com |Metro 1, 2, 3: Sol*

TIENDA BERNABÉU
(125 D3) (*Ⓜ 0*)
Everything that can have a logo printed on it is available in the Real Madrid fan shop located on the east side of the stadium – there is also an outlet near the Puerta del Sol *(Carmen 3)*. *C/ del Padre Damián 3 | Puerta 55 | Metro 10: Santiago Bernabéu*

TIENDA TORO DE OSBORNE
(128 C3) (*Ⓜ H2*)
It is probably the symbol of Spain: the black silhouetted image of a bull from the Andalusian sherry brand Osborne. This store housed in the Corte Inglés in Salamanca sells gifts and souvenirs with the original bull. *C/ de Serrano 47 | www.tiendaosborne.es | Metro 5: Rubén Darío*

TUNUNTUNUMBA
(123 E4) (*Ⓜ G5*)
A tiny treasure trove in Huertas specialising in the most original musical instruments from around the world especially drums, flutes and plucked instruments. *C/ Santa María 34 | www.tununtunumba.com | Metro 1: Antón Martín*

ENTERTAINMENT

CITY **WHERE TO START?**
Start your evening at the *terrazas* on the **Plaza Santa Ana** (Metro 2: Sevilla) then head to the tapas and music bars in **Huertas**, or, if you are the classic type, begin with an aperitif at the **Plaza Mayor** (Metro 1, 2, 3: Sol) followed by a stroll to **Cava Baja** where you will find so many tapas bars that it would be a shame to spend the evening in just one. Younger tourists should make a beeline for **Malasaña** where the **Plaza San Ildefonso** (Metro 1, 10: Tribunal) is a good point to start out from.

When do the Madrileños find time to sleep? There are traffic jams on the Gran Vía and throngs of people on Calle Huertas – at three in the morning! From Thursday evening to Sunday morning the city is constantly on the move, everyone is out and about in search of *marcha.* The word literally means to be on the march or to keep on going non-stop. *¿A dónde vamos ahora?* Where to now? This is the question heard over and over again throughout the evening as friends decide their next move on the *marcha.* The locals like to meet up in large groups to enjoy themselves, to have fun, laugh, drink, smoke and dance – and more often than not the driving force is *salir para ligar:* going out for the evening in order to find someone to hit it off with.

Nights are a celebration: no one stays at home at night – Madrid's night owls need to do the *marcha*

When the Spanish talk about bars they mean tapas bars or cafés, altough the concept of what we call pubs back home has now also caught on in Spain. They are also called pubs but the Spanish pronunciation sounds more like *paffs* so you may not recognise the word right away. Many of these pubs also have dance floors whereas a *discoteca* generally means there is an admission fee. To escape this Babylonian confusion, any nightlife venue that is a popular spot is simply called a *sitio de marcha*, or a happening place.

Becoming part of Madrid's nightlife is an easy matter of just joining in. Something that is even easier if you are staying in a central location: simply step out of your hotel door and you're right in the thick of things.

Each neighbourhood has its own nightlife centre: there is the Plaza Santa Ana in Huertas, the Calle Argumosa in Lavapiés, the Plaza Humilladero in La Latina, the Plazas Dos de Mayo and San Ildefonso in Malasaña, the Plaza Chueca in Chueca. Hot summer nights are spent on the

Atenas is the trendiest of Madrid's open air bars, known to the locals as *terrazas*

streets at the *terrazas* or outdoor bars. Madrileños certainly know how to enjoy life – they have a way of celebrating it as if there is no tomorrow – and even though it doesn't seem like it, they too welcome a good night's rest.

BARS, PUBS & TERRAZZAS

1862 DRY BAR (127 F4) (*Ω F3*)
The first book about cocktails is reputed to have been published in 1862, hence the name of this upmarket yet relaxed bar in Malasaña. *Mon–Sat 3.30pm–2am, Sun 3pm–10pm | C/ del Pez 27 | Metro 2: Noviciado*

CAFÉ GALDÓS (123 E2) (*Ω G4*)
Once a traditional café, now a meeting place for the intellectual crowd. Relaxed music still makes it easy to have conversations. Tapas, exhibitions, occasionally short films. *Mon–Fri 8am–1am, Sat/Sun 5pm–1am | C/ los Madrazo 10 | Metro 2: Sevilla*

CASA PUEBLO (123 E3) (*Ω F5*)
Warm and inviting bar that seems to have made a leap through time from the 1920s right into the present day. A piano stands at the ready for live performances, although more often than not you'll hear jazz recordings played. *Mon–Fr 5pm–2am, Sat/Sun 3pm–2am | C/ León 3 | Metro 1: Antón Martín*

CHOCOLATERÍA SAN GINÉS ★ ●
(122 C3) (*Ω E4*)
A nightly ritual: first hit Madrid's dance floors then when you've worked up a late night appetite, head here for *churros con chocolate*. First opened in 1894. *Daily 24 hrs | Pasadizo San Ginés 5 | Metro 1, 2, 3: Sol*

COCK (123 E2) (*Ω F4*)
A big hall that exudes a sort of faded and tired elegance. Mostly frequented by an older crowd that remain unperturbed by the rather disdainful waiters who are part

and parcel of the allure of the place. *Daily 4pm–3am | C/ Reina 16 | Metro 1, 5: Gran Vía*

COSTELLO (123 D2) (*ⁿⁿ F4*)

A funky café and club that draws a sophisticated crowd. Have a drink on the "Cocktail Floor" or opt for the live music in the basement. *Sun–Wed 8pm–3am, Thu–Sat 6pm–3.30am | C/ Caballero de Gracia 10 | www.costelloclub.com | Metro 1, 5: Gran Vía*

EL VIAJERO ☆ (122 B4) (*ⁿⁿ E5*)

This pub and restaurant in La Latina has a lovely rooftop terrace which is unfortunately far too overcrowded. *Tue–Thu 5pm–0.30am, Fri 3pm–1.30am, Sat noon–1.30am, Sun noon–0.30am | Plaza de la Cebada 11 | Metro 5: La Latina*

INSIDER TIP JOSEALFREDO (122 C1) (*ⁿⁿ E4*)

Cocktail bar whose sombre charm and retro look may not appeal to everyone. Still you'll find it packed to the hilt from midnight. *Daily 7pm–3am | C/ de Silva 22 | Metro 3, 5: Callao*

LA RECOBA (123 D4) (*ⁿⁿ F5*)

A quaint restaurant and bar on the edge of Lavapiés. If the owner takes a liking to you he will serenade you with a tango. Pizza served until three in the morning. *Tue–Sun 8pm–3am | C/ Magdalena 27 | Metro 1: Antón Martín*

LARIOS CAFÉ (118 B1) (*ⁿⁿ E4*)

The place and its patrons are just as cool as those in New York. Here you can dance the night away in the basement and still grab a late night bite in the restaurant area (*Moderate*) INSIDER TIP until 1.30am. *Tue–Thu 9pm–4am, Fri/Sat 9pm–6am | C/ de Silva 4 | www.larioscafe.com | Metro 2: Santo Domingo*

INSIDER TIP MARTÍNEZ BAR (123 D1) (*ⁿⁿ F4*)

A bar behind the Telefónica skyscraper with an inviting atmosphere with old furnishings, a wooden bar and an enormous selection of gins. Brunch on Sundays. *Mon–Sat 5pm–2.30am, Sun 1pm–1am | C/ del Barco 4 | Metro 1, 5: Gran Vía*

MUSEO CHICOTE (123 E2) (*ⁿⁿ F4*)

This is the most famous cocktail bar in the city. Its founder Pedro Chicote was a barman at the Ritz in 1931 and proud of his 10,000 bottles – hence the name "Museo". Today, they still have cocktails, a DJ and brunch on the weekends. *Tue–Fri 5pm–3.30 am, Sat 1.30pm–3.30am, Sun 1.30pm–9.30pm | Gran Vía 12 | www. museo-chicote.com | Metro 5: Gran Vía*

TERRAZA ATENAS ● (127 D6) (*ⁿⁿ D5*)

Madrid's trendiest open air bar where it's difficult to get served at the bar if you're there around 2am at night. Once you've paid for your expensive beer, sit down in the cool grass in the Parque de Atenas and

---

★ **Chocolatería San Ginés**
A Madrid ritual: tuck into *churros con chocolate* after a night of dancing → p. 76

★ **Casa Patas**
Madrid's most famous flamenco stage → p. 79

★ **Círculo de Bellas Artes**
Architectural gem, celebrated cultural centre and elegant café all in one → p. 81

★ **Café Central**
Top drawer jazz every night → p. 82

MARCO POLO HIGHLIGHTS

listen to the house music played by the resident DJ. *May–mid Sept daily 11am–3am | C/ de Segovia, corner Cuesta de la Vega | Metro 5, 6: Puerta del Ángel, La Latina*

CLUBS

BUT (128 A4) *(⍟ F3)*
The former Pachá is today the temple of the indie pop scene on Fridays and Satur-

Tue–Sat midnight–5.30am, concerts 10pm | admission fee 10 euros | C/ Jardines 3 | www.elsolmad.com | Metro 1, 5: Gran Vía

INDEPENDANCE CLUB (122 C4) *(⍟ F5)*
This indie club has gained a reputation as one of Madrid's trendiest discos in just a few years on the scene. *Thu–Sat 11.30pm–6am | admission from 5 euros |*

Joy Eslava is one of Madrid's oldest discos – right in the centre of Madrid

days (when it is the *Ocho y Medio Club*), while on Sun and Wed it opens for ballroom dancing. *Wed 10.30am–4pm, Fri/Sat 23.30pm–5.30am, Sun 18.30pm–midnight | admission 15 euros | C/ Barceló 11 | www.butmadrid.com | Metro 1, 10: Tribunal*

EL SOL (123 D2) *(⍟ F4)*
Madrid's most famous rock club and stage is a survivor of the 1980s *movida.*

C/ del Doctor Cortezo 1 | independance club.com | Metro 1: Tirso de Molina

JOY ESLAVA (122 C2) *(⍟ F4)*
An old veteran in Madrid's nightlife scene. Housed in the old Teatro Eslava here everybody who is anybody dances the night away to frenetic rhythms. *Daily 11.30pm–6am | admission from 10 euros | C/ de Arenal 11 | www.joy-eslava.com | Metro 1, 2, 3: Sol*

LA CARTUJA (123 D3) (*Ø F4*)

An unpretentious venue for an unpretentious crowd that wants nothing more than to dance the night away to Latino hits. *Wed–Sat 11pm–5.30am | admission 8 euros | C/ Cruz 10 | Metro 1, 2, 3: Sol, Sevilla*

TROPICAL HOUSE (122 C1) (*Ø E4*)

One of Madrid's largest salsa clubs. Its patrons are predominantly Latin American. *Fri/Sat midnight–6am, Sun 9pm–6am | admission 8 euros | Plaza de los Mostenses 11 | www.tropicalhouse.es | Metro 3, 10: laza de España*

FLAMENCO

At *www.deflamenco.com,* , click "Agenda" to find an up-to-date list of flamenco performances.

LAS CARBONERAS (122 B3) (*Ø E5*)

This *tablao* continues the tradition of the *cafés de cantantes* or "song cafés" that popularised the art of flamenco at the end of the 19th century. Its modern interior sets it apart from the usual tourist *tablaos*. The same goes for its repertoire, especially on weekends. *Dinner/show Mon–Thu 7.30pm/8.30pm and 10/10.30pm, Fri/Sat 7.30/8.30 and 10/11pm, Sun 7.30/8.30pm | dinner and show from 70* euros *| Plazuela del Conde de Miranda 1 | tel. 915 42 86 77 | www.tablaolascarboneras.com | Metro 2, 5: Ópera*

CASA PATAS ⭐ (123 D4) (*Ø F5*)

Still *the* flamenco restaurant in Madrid with pure flamenco performed live in a backroom. Tickets cost around 35 euros and should be booked two days in advance. *Programme starts 10.30pm Mon–Thu, 9pm and midnight Fri/Sat | C/ Cañizares 10 | tel. 913 69 04 96 | www.casapatas.com | Metro 1: Antón Martín*

CORRAL DE LA MORERÍA
(122 A4) (*Ø D5*)

Reservations are a must at Madrid's oldest *tablao* (established in 1956) in the vicinity of the Jardines de las Vistillas. *Shows 8.30 and 10.20pm, with dinner from 7/9.55pm | admission from 40 euros | C/ Morería 17 | tel. 913 65 84 46 | www.corraldelamoreria.com | Metro 5: La Latina*

INSIDER **TIP** ▶ LAS TABLAS
(122 A1) (*Ø D3*)

Two young flamenco dancers opened this *tablao* in 2003 and its shows are far less touristy than the older more established *tablaos*. *Shows daily 8pm and 10pm | admission from 27 euros | Plaza de España 9 | tel. 915 42 05 20 | www.lastab*

RELAX & ENJOY

● The Arabian *Hammam Al Andalus* **(122 C3) (*Ø F5*)** *(admission every 2 hours every day from 10am–midnight, by reservation only | bath with massage from 43 euros | C/ de Atocha 14 | tel. 9 14 29 90 20 | www.medinamayrit.com | Metro 1, 2, 3: Sol, Tirso de Molina)* invites guests to take a journey back in time to Spain's Moorish past. Get away from the city's noise and pollution for one and a half hours to bathe in the hot water pools under the hammam's stone arches in warm shades of orange. Finish the relaxation in style with a 15-minute poolside massage by a professional masseur.

Café Central – always a good bet for jazz fans

lasmadrid.com | Metro 3, 10: Plaza de España

TORRES BERMEJAS (122 C2) *(ⅅ F4)*

The late and great Camerón de la Isla made his debut in this *tablao* located in one of the side streets off from the Gran Vía (where he remained a resident artist for twelve years). He called the stage a "cathedral of flamenco". *Programme daily 9.10 and 10.50pm | admission 39 euros, with menu 72 euros | C/ de Mesonero Romanos 11 | torresbermejas.com | Metro 3, 5: Callao*

CINEMA

Madrid is a city of cinemas and on any given evening you can choose from about 70 films. Find out what's showing at *www. guiadelocio.com/madrid/cine.* Cinema tickets cost around 9 euro. Mainstream films are usually dubbed into Spanish but there are also many cinemas that specialise in screening originals with subtitles *(v.o.s.)*.

CINE CAPITOL ● (122 C1) *(ⅅ E4)*

The golden age of the Gran Vía with its cinemas lives on here today. Cinema 1 can seat 1350 people – an opera house of film. *Gran Vía 41 | Metro 3, 5: Callao*

PLAZA DE LOS CUBOS (127 E4) *(ⅅ E3)*

Over the years this small square near the Plaza de España has come into its own. There are three cinemas with 20 auditoriums showing the latest international box office hits in the original with Spanish subtitles. Right on the square is the

Princesa, through the passage to the Calle Martín de los Heros, there's the *Golem* (no. 14) and the *Renoir Plaza España* (no. 12). In true Hollywood Walk of Fame style, the names of 26 Spanish film stars – from Pedro Almodóvar to Concha Velasco - are embedded in the pavement in front of the cinemas. Opposite the cinema (no. 11), the book shop (with a cosy café) INSIDER TIP *Ocho y Medio* specialises in film literature. *Metro 3, 10: Plaza de España*

CULTURAL CENTRES

LA CASA ENCENDIDA (123 D6) *(𝄞 F6)*
The "enlightened house" was built more than a century ago as a modern bank but it looks more like a factory. After standing empty for many years it is now being used as a cultural centre with exhibitions, films, theatre, book readings and concerts. *Daily 10am–10pm | Ronda de Valencia 2 | www.lacasaencendida.es | Metro 3: Embajadores*

CÍRCULO DE BELLAS ARTES ★ ●
(123 E2) *(𝄞 G4)*
The "circle of fine arts" is housed in a magnificent 1926 building designed by Madrid architect Antonio Palacios and is the perfect setting for lectures, exhibitions and concerts. The café on the ground floor is excellent and well worth a visit despite the 1 euro entrance fee. An extra 2 euros gives you access to the ⚡ *azotea,* the roof terrace that has a wonderful view of Madrid. *Tue–Sun 11am–2pm and 5pm–9pm, café daily 9am–1am, azotea Mon–Fri 9am–9pm, Sat/Sun 11am–9pm | C/ de Alcalá 42 | www.circulobellasartes.com | Metro 2: Banco de España*

CONDE DUQUE (127 E3) *(𝄞 E2–3)*
The cultural centre in the 18th century barracks offers theatre, concerts and ex-

hibitions. *C/ Conde Duque 11 | Metro 3: Ventura Rodríguez*

MATADERO MADRID ★ ●
(132 A6) *(𝄞 F8)*
In 2007 this former slaughterhouse dating to 1924 was transformed by Madrid's city administration into a cultural centre and has gone on to become one of the most influential of its kind in Spain. The buildings have retained their industrial character of the early 20th century and are a perfect platform for theatre and concert performances, exhibitions and cinema showings. Next door to the *cineteca* is the restaurant 🍴 *Cantina (Tue–Sun noon–1am | Budget)* serving delicious vegetarian food. The events held at the Matadero are some of the most exciting on Madrid's cultural scene. *Tue–Fri 4pm–9pm, Sat/Sun 11am–9pm | Paseo de la Chopera 14 | www.mataderomadrid.org | Metro 3, 6: Legazpi*

LOW BUDGET

Spanish cinema for as little as 2.50 euros? Head for at the *Cine Doré* **(123 E4)** *(𝄞 F5) (Closed Mon C/ de Santa Isabel 3 | Metro 1: Antón Martín)* home to Filmothek – the state-run Spanish film library.

Free live rock performances are held six times a week at 12.30am in *Honkytonk* **(128 A3)** *(𝄞 G2) (Mon–Sat 9.30pm–5am | C/ Covarrubias 24 | Metro 4, 5, 10: Alonso Martínez).*

madridfree.com provides a list of free exhibitions, concerts, cinema showings and theatre performances.

LIVE MUSIC

CAFÉ CENTRAL ⭐ (123 D3) *(🛱 F5)*

Madrid's temple of jazz and alternative music genres as well as a plush yet cosy café – unfortunately for locals it is threatened with closure. *Daily 12.30pm–2.30am | admission 10–20 euros | Plaza del Ángel 10 | www.cafecentralmadrid.com | Metro 1, 2, 3: Sol*

CLAMORES (128 A3) *(🛱 F2)*

Some of Madrid's greatest jazz concerts take place in this huge basement club. *Daily 7pm–3am | admission 5–20 euros | C/ Alburquerque 14 | www.salaclamores.com | Metro 1, 4: Bilbao*

INSIDER TIP ► EL JUNCO (128 B4) *(🛱 G3)*

A tucked away popular live jazz venue. After the performance a DJ takes over until the early hours. *Tue–Sat 10pm–5.30am | admission 9 euros | Plaza Santa Bárbara 10 | www.eljunco.com | Metro 4, 5, 10: Alonso Martínez*

LIBERTAD 8 (123 E1) *(🛱 G4)*

"Freedom 8" café opened its doors in 1976, a few months after the death of Spanish dictator Franco. It is an institution of sorts and a venue for singer-songwriters and popular music of the more quiet variety. *Daily 4pm–2am | admission around 8 euros | C/ Libertad 8 | www.libertad8cafe.es | Metro 5: Chueca*

CAFÉ POPULART (123 E4) *(🛱 F5)*

Live jazz every evening from 10pm onwards. A classic in Huertas. *Daily 6pm–2.30am | free admission | C/ de las Huertas 22 | www.populart.es | Metro 1: Antón Martín*

OPERA, BALLET & CLASSICAL MUSIC

AUDITORIO NACIONAL DE MÚSICA (125 F4) *(🛱 O)*

The concert hall built in 1988 is the residence of the Spanish national orchestra

Royal performance from the stalls to the upper tiers: Madrid's opera house, Teatro Real

– Madrid's first port of call for classical music. *C/ del Príncipe de Vergara 146 | www.auditorionacional.mcu.es | Metro 9: Cruz del Rayo*

COMPAÑÍA NACIONAL DE DANZA

Spain's national ballet company launched an international star, the choreographer Nacho Duato (today the artistic director of the Berlin State Ballet). The productions by his successor José Carlos Martínez can be seen on various stages. Programme available at *cndanza. mcu.es*

TEATRO REAL

(122 B2) (*Ø E4*)

Madrid's Opera witnessed its heyday under the auspices of Gerard Mortier who died in 2014 yet the quality of music there is still impressive. *Plaza de Oriente | www.teatro-real.com | Metro 2, 5: Ópera*

TEATRO DE LA ZARZUELA

(123 E2) (*Ø G4*)

Zarzuela is a genre of Spanish theatre named after a royal palace close to Madrid which was famous for its festivities and incorporates operatic elements. This is its mecca. *C/ Jovellanos 4 | teatrodelazarzue la.mcu.es | Metro 2: Banco de España*

THEATRE & MUSICALS

CENTRO DRAMÁTICO NACIONAL MARÍA GUERRERO (128 B4) (*Ø G3*)

Madrid's most famous theatre on the outskirts of the Chuecas district. *C/ Tamayo y Baus 4 | cdn.mcu.es | Metro 4, 5: Colón, Chueca*

MUSICALS

Many of the old, glamorous cinemas along the Gran Vía have been transformed into musical theatres. The programme is available at *www.esmadrid. com/agenda-musicales.*

TEATRO ALFIL (127 F4) (*Ø F3*)

Small independent theatre in Malasaña which has perfected the art of comedy. *C/ del Pez 10 | teatroalfil.es | Metro 2: Noviciado*

TEATRO NUEVO APOLO

(123 D4) (*Ø F5*)

Spanish and foreign productions from all genres ranging from musicals, comedies and dance to theatre. *Plaza Tirso de Molina 1 | www.teatronuevoapolo.com | Metro 1: Tirso de Molina*

INSIDER TIP TEATROS DEL CANAL

(124 A6) (*Ø F1*)

Funded by the regional government, the theatre offers one of the city's most eclectic programmes: theatre, ballet and music. *C/ Cea Bermúdez 1 | www.teatros canal.com | Metro 2, 7: Canal.*

WHERE TO STAY

While middle-range hotels are few and far between, travellers on company business trips are spoilt for choice with around 250 hotels and well over 600 *hostales* with more than 80,000 beds to choose from.

Most hotels have at least three stars and are priced accordingly, even though they may not necessarily be on a par with those in Paris or New York. Always check the room rates when making your reservation as they are often cheaper than the official rates listed on their websites. It is also worth checking so-called specials that hotel agents offer on the Internet and ask directly at the hotel.

For tourists who cannot make tax deductions for their trip, finding a suitable hotel will be more difficult. Even very basic two

star hotels often charge more than 100 euros a night for a double room. Fortunately there is the alternative option offered by the *hostales* (guest houses). They are often converted apartments in the historic old town. They usually only occupy one or two floors and are generally privately run by married couples who have their own living quarters in a section of the *hostal*. For a long time these guest houses did not have a particularly good reputation. However, as Madrid became more affluent things changed. Guests have become more demanding and so the standards have improved accordingly. Most of the guest houses are regularly refurbished, a television set and air conditioning are no longer exceptions and it is now also common for rooms to have

It is easy to find a cheap hostel or a luxury hotel in Madrid – but accommodation in the middle price range is rather limited

their own en suite bathrooms. If all you need is a quiet place to sleep, with no added luxuries, then the *hostales* are a great option. Especially as you will seldom have to pay more than 70 euros a night.

HOTELS: EXPENSIVE

CATALONIA LAS CORTES
(123 E3) (*🕮 F5*)

This magnificent four-star hotel in Huertas is housed in an 18th century city palace near the Plaza Santa Ana. It is charmingly furnished with lovely antiques and features some restored ceiling frescoes. *65 rooms | C/ del Prado 6 | tel. 913 89 60 51 | www.catalonialascortes.com | Metro 1: Antón Martín*

HOTEL DE LAS LETRAS (123 D2) (*🕮 F4*)

Luxury four-star hotel on the Gran Vía which is also a popular haunt of Madrileños due to its exclusively located ☀ rooftop terrace. The walls of the elegant rooms with their understated deco are individually decorated with quotes by famous writers and poets. *109 rooms | Gran Vía 11 | tel. 9 71 99 80 60 | www. hoteldelasletras.com | Metro 1, 5: Gran Vía*

ME MADRID REINA VICTORIA
(123 D3) (*ω F5*)

Hip, modern and expensive. This old bull-fighter hotel on the Plaza Santa Ana is barely recognisable since its relaunch a few years ago. A home cinema and maxi bar replace the television set and minibar. *192*

tapas mile, the Cava Baja: Opened in 1868, this 19th century inn has been tastefully restored into a colourful boutique hotel which has retained its flair of the past. *27 rooms | C/ Cava Baja 14 | tel. 9 11 19 14 24 | www.posadadeldragon. com | Metro 5: La Latina*

SILKEN PUERTA AMÉRICA ★
(129 F1) (*ω K1*)

Fancy staying in a room designed by Zaha Hadid or Ron Arad? The 12 floors of this

Designers were given free reign in the Silken Puerta América

rooms | Plaza de Santa Ana 14 | tel. 917 01 60 00 | www.memadrid.com | Metro 1, 2, 3: Sol

INSIDER TIP ▶ POSADA DEL DRAGÓN
(122 F4) (*ω E5*)

One of Madrid's finest and most traditional accommodations located on the

hotel showcase contemporary architecture and design. Big names like Oscar Niemeyer, Arata Isozaki, David Chipperfield, Norman Foster are some of those that participated in its design. The 75 million euro project is located between the trade fair and the city centre, not the best location if you are a tourist but interesting for those on a business trip. *308 rooms | Av. de América 41 | tel. 917 44 54 00 | www.hotelpuer tamerica.com | Metro 7: Cartagena*

ÚNICO (128 C3) (*ⵉ H2*)

A black and white interior, decorated with stucco elements and elegant fabrics. The style of this boutique hotel fits perfectly into the upscale surroundings of the Salamanca district. Everything here is a tick better and more expensive than in other places. After an hour of relaxation in its wellness and spa facilities, treat yourself to a meal in Ramón Freixa's two-star restaurant. *44 rooms | C/ de Claudio Coello 67 | tel. 9 17 81 01 73 | www.unicoho telmadrid.com | Metro 4: Serrano*

HOTELS: MODERATE

ATENEO (121 D2) (*ⵉ F4*)

Affordable three star hotel in a restored 18th century townhouse next to the Puerta del Sol (but quite close to the red-light district). *38 rooms | C/ Montera 22 | tel. 915 21 20 12 | www.hotelateneo.es | Metro 1, 2, 3: Sol*

CENTRAL PALACE MADRID (122 B2) (*ⵉ E4*)

Small yet spacious almost luxury 3rd floor *hostal* at the Plaza de Oriente – some of the ⚹ rooms offer views of the Royal Palace. *6 rooms | Plaza de Oriente 2 | tel. 9 15 48 20 18 | centralpalace madrid.com | Metro 2, 5: Ópera*

INSIDER TIP MAIN STREET MADRID (122 C1) (*ⵉ E4*)

Centrally located on the 5th floor of one of the magnificent Gran Vía buildings, this hostal is elegantly furnished in a contemporary, minimalistic design. The rooms are small but offer guests a touch of luxury. Unbeatable value for money. *9*

Reina Victoria watches over the entrance to the Calderón de la Barca

rooms | Gran Vía 50 | tel. 9 15 48 18 78 | mainstreetmadrid.com | Metro 3, 5: Callao

ONE SHOT PRADO 23 (123 E3) (*ⵉ F5*)

Stylish, modern hotel at the heart of Huertas, with all comforts and surprising design touches. *42 rooms | C/ del Prado*

★ **The Westin Palace**
Not only a hotel but a Madrid institution
→ p. 88

★ **Silken Puerta América**
Its twelve floors showcase a whole world of design
→ p. 86

MARCO POLO HIGHLIGHTS

23 | tel. 9 14 20 40 01 | www.hoteloneshot prado23.com | Metro 1: Antón Martín

PRAKTIK METROPOL (128 A5) (*∅ F4*)
Brightly restored rooms in a fresh design just around the corner from the Gran Vía. The three ✂ INSIDER TIP *Gran Vía Corner* rooms with panoramic views are particularly appealing (and slightly more expensive). *60 rooms | C/ Montera 47 | tel. 9 15 21 29 35 | www.praktikmetropol.com | Metro 1, 5: Gran Vía*

ROOM MATE ALICIA (123 D3) (*∅ F5*)
This spectacular industrial building on the Plaza Santa Ana was built in the beginning of the 20th century. It is now a very trendy hotel with bright, pleasant rooms. *34 rooms | C/ del Prado 2 | tel. 913 89 60 95 | alicia.room-matehotels.com | Metro 1, 2, 3: Sol*

ROOM MATE MARIO
(122 B2) (*∅ E4*)
At a time when contemporary design was still considered a risk in Madrid this sophisticated yet intimate hotel opened up on the curved alleyway of Campomanes near the opera. The clean lines and generously proportioned rooms never fail to impress, nor does the excellent breakfast. *54 rooms | C/ Campomanes 4 | tel. 915 48 85 48 | mario.room-matehotels.com | Metro 2, 5: Ópera*

LUXURY HOTELS

AC Palacio del Retiro (128 C6) (*∅ H4*)
Opposite the Retiro, this has to be one of Madrid's most beautiful luxury boutique hotels. The listed building dates from the early 20th century and is perfectly complemented by a luxurious and contemporary interior. The spa offers a sauna, Jacuzzi and Turkish bath. *From 230 euros | 51 rooms | C/ de Alfonso XII 14 | tel. 915 23 74 60 | www.ac-hotels.com | Metro 2: Retiro*

Only You (123 E1) (*∅ G3*)
It's maybe the amazing location at the heart of Chueca which has made this lovingly restored and authentically decorated 19th century royal palace such a popular favourite among Madrid's hotels since its opening in 2013. *From 198 euros | 125 rooms | C/ Barquillo 21 | tel. 9 10 05 22 22 | www.onlyyouhotels.com | Metro 5: Chueca*

Ritz (123 F3) (*∅ G4*)
King Alfonso XIII felt that the then rather provincial Madrid needed its own Ritz so that it could be as cosmopolitan as Paris or London. In 1910 his wish came true. Today the hotel next to the Prado remains a favourite of visiting royalty and heads of state. *From 280 euros | 167 rooms | Plaza de la Lealtad 5 | tel. 917 01 67 67 | www.ritz.es | Metro 2: Banco de España*

The Westin Palace ⭐ **(123 E3)** (*∅ G5*)
Opened in 1912 the Palace is still Madrid's most famous hotel 100 years later. The big attraction was and is its massive stained glass dome on the ground floor. *Special offers from 265 euros, regular price from 330 euros | 466 rooms | Plaza de las Cortes 7 | tel. 913 60 80 00 | www.westinpalacemadrid.com | Metro 2: Banco de España*

Contemporary interior of the listed Palacio del Retiro

SIDORME FUENCARRAL 52
(128 A4) (*F3*)

Opened in 2015, this hotel offers functional charm and a small, elegant rooftop terrace. Best location between Chueca and Malasaña. *44 rooms | C/ de Fuencarral 52 | tel. 9 02 02 31 20 (*) | www.sidorme.com | Metro 1, 10: Tribunal*

HOTELS & HOSTALES: BUDGET

COMERCIAL (122 C3) (*F5*)

Marvellously cosy *hostal* ideally located next to the Plaza Mayor. Some rooms share a bathroom. **INSIDER TIP** Very affordable if you are travelling on your own. *11 rooms | C/ de Esparteros 12 | tel. 915 22 66 30 | www. hostalcomercial.com | Metro 1, 2, 3: Sol*

FLAT 5 (127 F4) (*E3*)

On the fifth floor of no. 55 in the Calle San Bernardo, this modern, colourful *hostal* awaits you with nice details. Idel location for night owls wanting to discover Malasaña and Conde Duque. *9 rooms | C/ San Bernardo 55 | tel. 9 11 27 24 00 | flat5madrid.com | Metro 2: Noviciado*

HOSTAL ABRIL (123 D1) (*F3*)

Lovingly restored in vibrant colours, this 4th floor *hostal* on the Calle de Fuencarral in the centre of Madrid is not the quietest accommodation available. *11 rooms | C/ de Fuencarral 39 | tel. 915 31 53 38 | www. hostalabrilmadrid.com | Metro 1, 5: Gran Vía*

HOSTAL ESMERALDA (123 D3) (*F4*)

This well-run *hostal* is managed by a friendly couple on the outskirts of Huertas, not far from the Puerta del Sol. *19 rooms | C/ Victoria 1 | tel. 915 21 00 77 | hresmeralda.net | Metro 1, 2, 3: Sol*

Hotel Plaza Mayor: reserve the penthouse suite!

HOSTAL MAYOR (122 C3) (*M F4*)

Cosy, well-maintained *hostal* with rooms at unbeatable prices just 50m away from the Puerta del Sol. The noise from Madrid's nightlife below occasionally drifts up to the 3rd floor. *11 rooms | C/ Mayor 5 | tel. 915 22 61 82 | www.hostalmayormadrid.com | Metro 1, 2, 3: Sol*

HOSTAL MONTALOYA (122 C4) (*M F5*)

Centrally located opposite the Teatro Nuevo Apolo, simple but creatively furnished, parquet floors. Friendly staff. *30 rooms | Plaza Tirso de Molina 20 | tel. 913 60 03 05 | www.hostalmontaloya.com | Metro 1: Tirso de Molin*

PLAZA MAYOR (122 C3) (*M F5*)

Located near Plaza Mayor, the rooms of this nice small hotel are unexciting but clean and comfortable. The suite takes up the entire top floor and has its own small terrace. *35 rooms | C/ de Atocha 2 | tel. 913 60 06 06 | www.h-plazamayor.com | Metro 1, 2, 3: Sol*

INSIDER TIP URBAN SEA ATOCHA (123 F5) (*M G5*)

Pretty rooms in a bright, fresh design, rooftop terrace and perfect location for art aficionados: The Reina Sofía, Prado, Caixaforum and Thyssen-Bornemisza are literally a stone's throw away. *36 rooms | C/ de Atocha 113 | tel. 913 69 28 95 | www.blueseahotels.com | Metro 1: Atocha*

APARTMENT HOTELS

If you're looking for an apartment, check out the offers at *www.atraveo.es, chic-rentals.com, www.friendlyrentals.com* or *www.only-apartments.es*.

INSIDER TIP NEW POINT MADRID (123 D2) (*M F4*)

Attractive apartment hotel close to the Gran Vía with modern yet cosily decorated rooms with parquet flooring and a small, intimate rooftop terrace. *24 apartments | C/ Montera 43 | tel. 910 05 22 06 | www.newpointmadrid.com | Metro 1, 5: Gran Vía | Moderate*

PRÍNCIPE 11 (123 D3) (*F5*)

Apartments and comfortable rooms with kitchenettes in a beautiful townhouse right in the middle of bustling Huertas. *36 apartments, studios and suites | C/ del Príncipe 11 | tel. 914 29 44 70 | www.at principe11.com | Metro 2: Sevilla | Budget– Moderate*

SERCOTEL SUITES VIENA
(127 D4) (*D3*)

Modern, unpretentious hotel situated close to the Plaza de España and the Templo de Debod. Spacious suites with comfortable beds and small kitchenettes. Excellent value for money. *57 suites | C/ Juan Álvarez Mendizábal 17 | tel. 917 58 36 05 | www.suitesviena.com | Metro 3: Ventura Rodríguez | Moderate*

SPLENDOM SUITES GRAN VÍA
(123 D1) (*F4*)

This new luxury apartment hotel housed behind a historic façade is located in a small side street off the Calle de Fuencarral. The rooms all feature balconies and are lovingly decorated in baroque style. *26 apartments | C/ San Onofre 5 | tel. 915 319 0 68 | www. splendomsuitesmadrid.com | Metro 1, 5: Gran Vía | Expensive*

YOUTH HOSTELS

THE HAT ⓦ (122 C3) (*E5*)

Housed in a royal palace of the 19th century and located just a few steps from the Plaza Mayor, this bright hostel with vibrant deco focuses on sustainability with its biomass heating and green standards. The staff provides information and advice on what to see and do in Madrid and the hotel has an intimate rooftop terrace snuggled between the old city's red-tiled roofs. Unfortunately booked out months in advance. *208 beds in 36 dorms and 6 double rooms | from 19.50 euros/person incl. breakfast, double room 70 euros | C/ Imperial 9 | tel. 917 72 85 72 | thehatmadrid. com | Metro 1: Tirso de Molinas*

SANTA CRUZ DE MARCENADO
(127 F3) (*E2*)

This state-run youth hostel near the Conde Duque cultural centre is great value for money. Only for tourists travelling on their own, you can only stay a maximum six nights. Rooms have four, six or eight beds. With a Youth Hostel Pass it is 19.80 euros including breakfast, 15.40 euros if you are 25–30 years old, 14 euros if you are under 25. *72 beds | C/ Santa Cruz de Marcenado 28 | tel. 915 47 45 32 | www.hihostels.com | Metro 3: Argüelles*

LOW BUDGET

The magnificent *Cat's Hostel* **(123 D4)** *(F5) (186 beds in 19 dormitories and 6 double rooms | from 16.50 euros/person including breakfast | C/ Cañizares 6 | tel. 913 69 28 07 | catshostel.com | Metro 1: Antón Martín)* is housed in an 18th century city palace in a quiet area near the Plaza Santa Ana. Its Moorish courtyard is worthy of a luxury hotel.

The *Posada de Huertas* **(123 D4)** *(G5) (152 beds in 22 dormitories and 7 double rooms | C/ de las Huertas 21 | tel. 914 29 55 26 | www. posadadehuertas.com | Metro 1: Antón Martín)* is in a typical Madrid apartment building from the 19th century. Accommodation starts at 17 euros per person including breakfast.

DISCOVERY TOURS

 ①

MADRID AT A GLANCE

START: **①** Miranda
END: **⑫** Chocolatería San Ginés

Distance:
🚶 10.6 km/6.5 mi, of which 8.5 km/5 mi on foot

20 hours
Walking time
(without stops)
2 hours

COSTS: approx. 100 euros (food and drink, taxi rides, admission to **②** Prado and **⑪** Joy Eslava)

IMPORTANT TIPS: purchase your entrance tickets to the **②** Prado in advance online at www.entradasprado.com. Although you are charged a 1 euro booking fee, it saves you queuing.

This route is intended for tourists with just 24 hours in Madrid and who don't want to miss any of the highlights. This tour of Madrid takes in city life, art, parks, a stroll through the royal palace gardens and old city as well as the best food and drink. It finishes the day in style with a dip into Madrid's nightlife!

Cities have many faces. If you want to get behind the scenes to explore their unique charm and head off the beaten track or find your way to green oases, handpicked restaurants or the best local activities, then these tailored Discovery Tours are just the right thing. Choose the best route for the day and follow in the footsteps of the MARCO POLO authors — well-prepared to navigate your way to all the many highlights that await you along the tour.

09:00am Start your day with a Spanish breakfast at the trendy ❶ Miranda *(daily | C/ de las Huertas 29 | Metro 1: Antón Martín)* in the centre of Madrid's poet district, Barrio de Huertas, named after the many writers and poets who lived there. **Stroll down the pedestrian precinct Huertas** where you will see literary quotes embossed in the paving and the Convento de las Trinitarias on your left where Cervantes was laid to rest. **At the end of the Calle de las Huertas cross the Paseo del Prado and head left up the road.**

❶ Miranda

1 Chamberí

Calle de Sta Engracia

Calle de Sagasta

Glorieta de Quévedo

Calle de A. Aguilera

Paseo E. Dato

Paseo de la Castellana

Cuartel del Conte Duque

Po. de Rosales

Calle de la Princesa

Centro

Paseo de Recoletos

Biblioteca Nacional Mus. Arqueol.

Paseo de Florida

8

Palacio del Senado

Gran Vía

11 **6**

Pl. de Cibeles **5**

4 Calle de O'Donnell

Parque

Calle de Bailén

Palacio Real

✝

7 **12**

Pl. Mayor

Calle de Alcalá

Paseo del Prado

3

del Retiro

10 **1**

Calle

✝

Basílica S. Francisco El Grande

9

Calle de Atocha

2

Museo del Prado

Palacio de Cristal

Retiro

Ronda de Toledo

Ronda de Atocha

de la Cabeza

Paseo de las Delicias

Av. Ciudad

1 km

0.62 mi

Emb

Estación de Atocha

| **2 Prado** | 🏛 |

10:00am On your right is the main entrance to the **2 Prado → p. 30**, where you can spend the next few hours admiring one of the world's finest collections by Hieronymus Bosch, Diego de Velázquez, Francisco de Goya, El Greco, Albrecht Dürer and many more besides.

01:00pm After your visit to the Prado, **head down the Calle Felipe IV and through the splendid Puerta de Felipe IV to enter** Madrid's green belt, the spacious **3 Parque del Retiro → p. 36**. After a short stroll around the gardens you'll reach the **Estanque** where you can watch the comings and goings around this artificial lake (or more like a large pond!) at the Plaza de Honduras garden café.

| **3 Parque del Retiro** | |

02:00pm **Leave the Retiro through the north-west corner of the park at the Puerta de la Independencia next to the Puerta de Alcalá. Now proceed down the Calle de Alcalá to the** ❹ **Plaza de Cibeles** → p. 33 with a photo opportunity of the Cybele fountain and the ornately designed Palacio de Cibeles which today houses the city hall. **Continue down the Calle de Alcalá with the landmark Metrópolis building in front of you** which also marks the start of the city's expansive ❺ **Gran Vía** → p. 42. **Take a stroll up this boulevard until you reach the Plaza de Callao** and the El Corte Inglés department store where you can enjoy your lunch and an amazing view over Madrid at the store's ninth floor restaurant, ❻ **Gourmet Experience Gran Vía** → p. 61.

05:00pm Go down the bustling shopping mile **Calle Preciados to the Puerta del Sol, the heart of Madrid and Spain's symbolic centre, turn right into the Calle Mayor and then take the first left along the Calle Postas to the Plaza Mayor.** If you are ready for a break, **continue down the Calle Mayor, past the Plaza de la Villa and go right along the Calle de Bailén to number 19:** take a seat outside ❼ **Anciano Rey de los Vinos** *(closed Tue)*, where you can try the restaurant's INSIDERTIP famous vermouth and admire the view of the La Almudena Cathedral.

07:00pm The bombastic Palacio Real stands just next door (leave a visit for another time) at the Plaza de Oriente which is full of street buskers and living statues at this time of the day. **Continue along the Calle de Bailén, past the Plaza de España and then take a left uphill to the** ❽ **Templo de Debod** → p. 45 – with a bit of luck, you'll be treated to a spectacular sunset.

09:00pm Expect to have worked up an appetite after all this walking. **So take a taxi to** ❾ **Cava Baja** → p. 65, Madrid's old town restaurant mile lined with tapas bars. Follow the locals and enjoy the evening "tapas hopping" for example **at number 26** in **Taberna Txakolina** *(daily | Moderate)*.

11:00pm A short stroll takes you to the heart of Madrid's nightlife, Huertas, to the ❿ **Plaza de Santa Ana** → p. 28. The only challenge will be to find a free table at one of the many street cafés.

❹ Plaza de Cibeles

❺ Gran Vía

❻ Gourmet Experience Gran Vía

❼ Anciano Rey de los Vinos

❽ Templo de Debod

❾ Cava Baja

❿ Plaza de Santa Ana

02:00am Want to dance? Madrid is still in full swing so why not make the most of your evening and **head along the Puerta del Sol and the Calle de Arenal** to one of the city's most famous discos ⑪ **Joy Eslava** → p. 78.

⑪ Joy Eslava

05:00am Just a few steps further is a famous institution ⑫ **Chocolatería San Ginés** → p. 76. which is open around the clock serving churros, deep-fried pastries, which are dipped into a thick hot chocolate sauce – what better way to round off a night on the town?

⑫ Chocolatería San Ginés

2
MADRID RÍO: ALONG THE CITY'S RIVERBANKS

START: ❶ Puerta del Sol END: ❶ Puerta del Sol	6 hours Cycling time (without stops) around 2 hours
Distance: 🚲 24 km/15 miles	

COSTS: 12 euros for bike hire, approx. 40 euros for food
WHAT TO PACK: water

IMPORTANT TIPS: bike hire → p. 111
Although the sight of cyclists in the Spanish capital is not as unusual as it used to be, you still need to have your wits about you in the city traffic. Madrid is hillier than you'd think so you need to be in a reasonably fit condition to tackle the city by bike.

This route takes you by bike away from the heat of the city and out into green open space with the Madrid Río parkland left and right of the Manzanares River to the city's forest Casa de Campo – and into the wilderness in the northwest of the city.

❶ Puerta del Sol

Your tour starts at the ❶ **Puerta del Sol**. Cycle down the Calle Mayor, cross the Calle de Bailén and at the cathedral take the winding and steep downhill road to the bottom where you turn left into the Ronda de Segovia. Continue straight along the cycling lane on the Paseo de los Melancólicos where you stay, even though the cycling lane bears off left into another street. As soon as you see the Estadio Vicente Calderón in front of you, Atlético Madrid's football stadium, **turn right into the small street San Alejandro where at the end you will spot a small sign pointing to the "Salón de Pinos":** you have already reached the park on the banks of the Manzanares, ❷ **Madrid Río**. Enjoy a short break at the river to take in the view of the stadium where you'll notice ⏹INSIDER**TIP** the motorway running underneath the stadium's stand.

Now cross the river over the Puente Principado de Andorra and turn left: cycle down river, taking a right along the Travesía Iván de Vargas and then a left into the Paseo de la Ermita del Santo. After a short steep uphill stretch, you will reach the entrance to the cemetery ❸ INSIDER TIP Cementerio de San Isidro. Take a stroll on foot around the cemetery, walking through the rows upon rows of splendid aristocratic gravestones while enjoying views stretching out to the Sierra de Guadarrama mountains.

Head back to the river (this time along the Calle San Ambrosio) and cycle leisurely along the river bank boulevard to the magnificent 16th century Renaissance bridge ❹ Puente de Segovia where you can stop to admire the beautiful view over the river to the Plaza de Espana towers, the royal palace and the cathedral. **Your route now takes you up river until you reach the Café del Río on your left. Behind the café is the wall of the ❺ Huerta de la Partida**, a garden of fruit trees established in the 16th century **which you now cycle through, keeping to the main path. When you reach the end of the garden, turn right and then left again into the countrified Paseo del Embarcadero.**

You will reach the Lago Casa de Campo **after just 400 m/130 ft. Cycle along the west banks of the lake** with its many garden restaurants and take a break at one of them such as ❻ **Urogallo** (closed Mon | Moderate). The restaurant is extremely busy at weekends so be prepared to be patient with the waiters.

Now continue around the lake to its north banks until you reach a road with a wide cycling lane, the Paseo del Piñonero, where you then take a left. Now cycle under

❷ Madrid Río

❸ Cementerio de San Isidro

❹ Puente de Segovia

❺ Huerta de la Partida

❻ Urogallo

The cycling lanes along Madrid Río are a dream in a city otherwise known as a cyclists' nightmare

the shade of the pine trees straight on and at the roundabout follow the cycling trail signposted "Senda Real GR 124". After approx. 1 km/0.6 mile you'll cross under a train track and then take the first right to cross the Carretera de Castilla over a cycling bridge.

Your route now takes you along the banks of the Manzanares. The river now resembles a small stream flowing into its natural bed and is surrounded by dense vegetation. After 2.5 km/1.6 mile along the river, the cycling lane crosses over two motorways in quick succession with the Manzanares River flowing in between.

Take a right at the end of the second bicycle bridge (signpost directing you to "Ciudad Universitaria") and follow an unpaved section which runs next to the motorway. Shortly afterwards take a right onto the pedestrian bridge leading over the next motorway. Follow the path past the university's veterinary faculty until you reach an entrance gate to the Moncloa Palace – the seat of the Spanish government. Bear right along a path where you'll be forgiven for thinking it is a dried-up river bed. Keep going though because it will take you back to the centre of Madrid.

DISCOVERY TOURS

You will come out at a large roundabout, bear left to cross the Avenida de Séneca and then follow the road signposted "Calle Cortada" (cul-de-sac) where you enter the Parque de la Bombilla. **Head straight on for 1 km/0.6 mile until you are standing in front of two chapels:** the one standing in the background is the **7 Ermita de San Antonio** → p. 53, where Goya is buried. Right next door is the **8 Casa Mingo** → p. 63, a culinary landmark in Madrid serving grilled chicken and Asturian *sidra.*

Now cross the Paseo de la Florida and take a left in front of the romantic Puente de la Reina Victoria into the Calle Aniceto Marinas which takes you back along the river to the Madrid Río park. Take a break at the **9 Ermita de la Virgen del Puerto** on your left and, in the trees, keep a look out for the INSIDER TIP green monk parakeets, a breed of parrot which has become almost a plague in Madrid.

Then take a left along the Calle de Segovia with a good 1 km/0.6 mile uphill stretch. The 10 Café del Nuncio → p. 57 is waiting for you on the right where you can enjoy a relaxing drink before rolling back down to the **1 Puerta del Sol**.

7 Ermita de San Antonio

8 Casa Mingo

9 Ermita de la Virgen del Puerto

10 Café del Nuncio

1 Puerta del Sol

3 CRAFTWORK AND GARDEN DESIGN

START: **1** Retiro Metro station
END: **12** The Westin Palace

Distance:
6.5 km/4 miles

7 hours
Walking time
(without stops)
1½ hours

COSTS: 1.50 euros for the boat trip, 4 euros admission to the **8** carpet museum, food approx. 25 euros, coffee and *horchata* approx. 11 euros

Discover Madrid's relaxing side right next to the hustle and bustle of the old town: this walking tour takes you through the Retiro city park, the botanical gardens and to the royal carpet factory.

❶ Retiro Metro station

❷ Estanque

❸ equestrian statue of Alfonso XII

❹ Palacio de Velázquez

❺ Palacio de Cristal

❻ Rosaleda

❼ Fuente del Ángel Caído

❽ Real Fábrica de Tapices

❾ Atocha station

From the ❶ **Retiro Metro station a pedestrian tunnel leads you under the Calle de Alcalá** to the heart of Madrid's largest park, the **Parque del Retiro → p. 36**. Stroll over to the ❷ **Estanque → p. 104** – where you can enjoy a trip on the solar-powered boat around the park's "pond". After your boat trip, head over **to the east banks of the Estanque** to the monumental ❸ **equestrian statue of Alfonso XII**. Take a break and join the crowds of young people hanging around the steps of the monument.

The ❹ Palacio de Velázquez stands in the park's south area. The palace houses a branch of the Museo Reina Sofía and exhibits contemporary art for free. Now take time out for a *horchata* in the garden café **next door. Continue on just 100 m/328 ft** to reach the glass dome of the ❺ **Palacio de Cristal** a palace also offering a free art exhibition.

The Paseo Julio Romero de Torres now leads you to ❻ Rosaleda, Retiro's 100-year rose garden. Now head **along the Paseo de Uruguay** to the intriguing statue of Lucifer ❼ **Fuente del Ángel Caído. Turn left along the Paseo Fernán Núñez and as soon as you reach the exercise equipment on your right, take a right heading downhill. When you reach the bottom, take a left and then the first right along a narrow path which leads you down a stone staircase and out of the park.**

Proceed down the Avenida Menéndez y Pelayo, along the Calle de Gutenberg to the Calle Fuenterrabía where in house number 2 you'll find the ❽ INSIDER TIP Real Fábrica de Tapices *(Mon–Fri 10am–2pm | C/ Fuenterrabía 2 | www.realfabricadetapices.com),* the royal carpet factory founded in 1721. Here you can watch how the factory's historic looms are used to hand weave tapestries using patterns by Goya.

Cross the Avenida Ciudad de Barcelona and follow the road on your right to the ❾ Atocha station → p. 46. At the entrance signposted "Salidas" (departures) you'll enter the tropical gardens where you can soak up the atmosphere while enjoying lunch at the **Samarkanda → p. 47** restaurant.

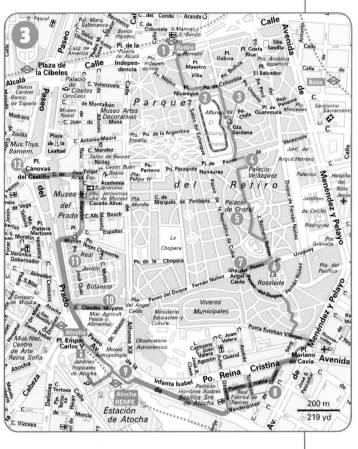

At the entrance to the Paseo del Prado take a quick detour to the ⑩ **Cuesta de Moyano**, where you can browse through the stands of antique books. **Then take a stroll up the Paseo del Prado and visit the ⑪ Real Jardín Botánico → p. 35 on your right. From the Calle Ruiz de Alarcón at the rear of the Prado museum, turn left along the Calle Felipe IV and** take a peak into the hotel ⑫ **The Westin Palace → p. 88**, where you can enjoy a posh coffee sat under the brightly coloured glass dome – a popular photo opportunity for tourists.

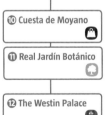

⑩ Cuesta de Moyano 🛍️

⑪ Real Jardín Botánico 🎧

⑫ The Westin Palace ☕

TAPAS AND TILES

START: ① Metrostation Quevedo
END: ⑫ Café El Mar

Distance:
➡ 5 km/3.1 miles

4 hours
Walking time
(without stops)
1½ hours

COSTS: approx. 40 euros for food and drink

IMPORTANT TIPS: programme of cultural centre exhibitions available at *www.condeduquemadrid.es*

This tour takes you almost without noticing from one district of Madrid to another, exploring small shops and restaurants whose facades or interiors are all lovingly decorated in tiles.

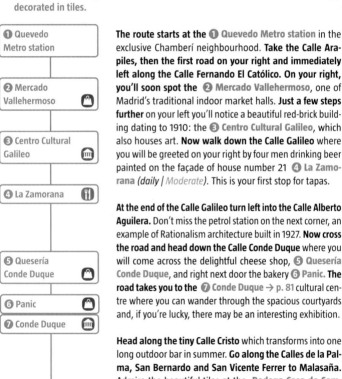

① Quevedo
Metro station

② Mercado
Vallehermoso

③ Centro Cultural
Galileo

④ La Zamorana

⑤ Quesería
Conde Duque

⑥ Panic

⑦ Conde Duque

⑧ Farmacia Juanse

The route starts at the ① **Quevedo Metro station** in the exclusive Chamberí neighbourhood. **Take the Calle Arapiles, then the first road on your right and immediately left along the Calle Fernando El Católico. On your right, you'll soon spot the** ② **Mercado Vallehermoso**, one of Madrid's traditional indoor market halls. **Just a few steps further** on your left you'll notice a beautiful red-brick building dating to 1910: the ③ **Centro Cultural Galileo**, which also houses art. **Now walk down the Calle Galileo** where you will be greeted on your right by four men drinking beer painted on the façade of house number 21 ④ **La Zamorana** *(daily | Moderate)*. This is your first stop for tapas.

At the end of the Calle Galileo turn left into the Calle Alberto Aguilera. Don't miss the petrol station on the next corner, an example of Rationalism architecture built in 1927. **Now cross the road and head down the Calle Conde Duque** where you will come across the delightful cheese shop, ⑤ **Quesería Conde Duque**, and right next door the bakery ⑥ **Panic. The road takes you to the** ⑦ **Conde Duque → p. 81** cultural centre where you can wander through the spacious courtyards and, if you're lucky, there may be an interesting exhibition.

Head along the tiny Calle Cristo which transforms into one long outdoor bar in summer. **Go along the Calles de la Palma, San Bernardo and San Vicente Ferrer to Malasaña.** Admire the beautiful tiles at the **Bodega Casa do Compañeiro** (number 44), even more splendid ones at the **Antigua Huevería** and the most stunning at the ⑧ **Farma-**

cia Juanse, a closed-down pharmacy which still advertises medicines from the late 19th century.

A little further at Calle Colón 13 is the ⑨ **Bodega La Ardosa** *(daily | Moderate)* with beer and delicious *salmorejo* among the tiled walls. **When you reach the end of the Calle Colón, turn right into the** ⑩ **Calle de Fuencarral** → p. 67 – an ideal place for window shopping **– and walk over the Puerta del Sol and Plaza Mayor to** ⑪ **Cava Baja** → p. 65, Madrid's tapas mile. The tile-covered façade of **La Chata** at number 24 is your next port of call on the tapas route.

Head back a few metres via the Calle San Bruno/Calle Estudios to the Plaza Cascorro. From there, walk down the Calle Embajadores. Stop at number 31 to see a barber at work on the painted tiles and then enjoy dinner at INSIDER TIP one of Madrid's finest vegetarian restaurants, the ⑫ **Café El Mar** *(daily | Budget)*.

⑨ Bodega La Ardosa 🍴

⑩ Calle de Fuencarral 🛍

⑪ Cava Baja 🍴

⑫ Café El Mar 🍴

The cheek-by-jowl tapas bars along the Cava Baja

TRAVEL WITH KIDS

AQUOPOLIS (134 B2) (*Ø 0*)
One of Europe's largest waterparks situated 30 km/19 miles outside Madrid with wave pool and spectacular water slides. It also offers a more laid back option with its mini golf course. Unfortunately the park is often overcrowded. *Mid-June–start of Sept Mon–Fri noon–7pm, Sat/Sun noon–8pm | 24.95 euros, children under 140 cm 19.50 euros, discounts available online | Villanueva de la Cañada | Av. Dehesa | takes 45 min. by bus 627 from the underground bus station Moncloa (Metro 3, 6: Moncloa) | villanueva.aquopolis.es*

CHURROS CON CHOCOLATE
Treat your children and yourself to this deliciously sweet speciality. Keep a look out for bars and *cafeterías* with the sign "Hay churros" outside. *Churros* are thin fluted dough strips or spirals that are deep-fried and then dipped in a cup of thick warm chocolate. Heavenly!

ESTANQUE ● (129 D6) (*Ø H4*)
Let yourself be ferried over the rectangular lake in the Retiro park on a solar-powered excursion boat or do it yourself in a rowing boat. *Daily 10am–2pm and 4pm–sunset (rowing boats all day) | solar boat 1.50 euros, rowing boat Mon–Fri 5.80 euros, Sat/Sun 7.50 euros | Metro 2: Retiro*

FAUNIA (0) (*Ø 0*)
A slightly different zoo: instead of animal enclosures there are complete habitats, from a tropical forest to a polar ecosystem. Discover 300 animal species on a five-hour walking tour. *March–Sept daily, Feb Sat/Sun 10am–sunset | admission 26 euros, children (3–7 years) 20 euros, discounts on the website | Av. Comunidades 28 | faunia.es | Metro 9: Valdebernardo*

MUSEO DE CERA (128 B–C4) (*Ø G3*)
Madrid's wax museum has all the Spanish and international icons: Pablo Picasso, Albert Einstein, King Felipe, George Clooney, Cristiano Ronaldo... Younger children can look forward to seeing Little Red Riding Hood or Spiderman. Resemblances to the originals is a matter of luck. *Mon–Fri 10am–2.30pm and 4.30pm–8.30pm, Sat/Sun 10am–8.30pm | admission 17 euros, children (4–12 years) 12 euros | Paseo de Recoletos 41 | www.museoceramadrid.com | Metro 4: Colón*

This large city is also fun for little people so take time out from your Madrid sightseeing and follow these few tips

MUSEO DEL FERROCARRIL
(132 B–C 4–5) (*Ⓜ G7*)
Las Delicias railway station was openend in 1880 but today the mighty iron and glass building serves as train museum. It showcases some 30 steam and diesel locomotives. Model train displays and little houses are also historic. *Tue–Fri 9.30am–3pm, Sat/Sun 10am–3pm, closed second half of Aug | admission 6 euros, children (4–12 years) 4 euros, Sun children and adults 2.50 euros | Paseo Delicias 61 | www.museodelferrocarril.org | Metro 3: Delicias*

PARQUE DE ATRACCIONES
CASA DE CAMPO (0) (*Ⓜ 0*)
This amusement park on the southern border of the Casa de Campo city forest still retains some of its 1960s charm. *Mid Sept–April mostly Sat/Sun only, May Wed–Sun, June–beginning Sept daily noon–dark | admission 31.90 euro, children (90–120 cm/2.9–3.9ft) 24.90 euro, discounts on the website | parquedeatracciones.es | Metro 10: Batán*

TELEFÉRICO ⬤ ☌ (126 C3) (*Ⓜ C2*)
The ten-minute cable car ride from the slopes of the Parque del Oeste to the heart of the Casa de Campo park belongs to one of Madrid's classic attractions which offers spectacular views of the park and city. *Oct–mid-March usually only runs on Sat/Sun, otherwise daily from noon to nightfall | return trip 5.75 euros | Paseo del Pintor Rosales/C/ Buen Suceso | teleferico.com | Metro 3, 4, 6: Argüelles*

ZOO AQUARIUM (0) (*Ⓜ 0*)
The zoo at the Casa de Campo city forest is one of Europe's most important with 4000 animals and 500 different species. There is also a dolphin pool, a sea lion enclosure, a tropical aquarium with 35 tanks and an aviary with 60 species of bird. Dolphin, sea lion, birds of prey and parrot shows are held and there is a petting zoo. *Daily 11am–at least 6pm, May–Aug 10.30am–at least 8pm | admission 22.95 euros, children (3–7 years) 18.60 euros | zoomadrid.com | Metro 5, 10: Casa de Campo*

FESTIVALS & EVENTS

EVENTS

5 JANUARY
Cabalgata de Reyes: Procession of the Three Wise Men, watched by the children.

MID-FEBRUARY
Arco international art fair at the Ifema trade fair grounds. *www.arco.ifema.es*

MAUNDY THURSDAY/GOOD FRIDAY
Semana Santa processions through the old town re-enact the Passion of Christ.

APRIL
Rock 'n Roll Madrid Maratón: 15,000 people take part in the city marathon, 9000 in the half marathon, while along the runners' way, rock bands make noise and ensure a great atosphere. *es.com petitor.com/madrid*

MID-APRIL–BEGINNING OF MAY
Festimad 2 M: Madrid's most important rock festival with concerts at several venues. *festimad.es*

MAY
2 May: *Comunidad de Madrid:* public holiday commemorates the rebels who resisted Napoleon's troops in 1808.

8–15 May: the city celebrates its saint ● *San Isidro*. Bullfights at the Las Ventas arena, folklore, music stages.

LATE MAY–BEGINNING OF JUNE
Feria del Libro in the Retiro: a two-week book fair with Spanish-speaking authors participating in book signing sessions. *www.ferialibromadrid.com*

JUNE–AUGUST
Photo-España: the whole city transforms itself into a huge photo exhibition. *www.phe.es*

23/24 JUNE
Noche de San Juan: On Midsummer Night Madrileños leap over fires, e.g. on the Plaza Dos de Mayo.

END OF JUNE/BEGINNING OF JULY
INSIDER TIP ▶ *Día del Orgullo Gay:* the gay pride parade in and around Chueca has become Madrid's largest street festival. *www.madridorgullo.com*

JULY
Frinje Madrid: the most daring and innovative festival of stage arts held in Matadero, the cultural centre in the old slaughterhouse. Meeting point of avant-

gardes from theatre, dance and circus. *www.frinjemadrid.com*

JULY/AUGUST
Veranos de la Villa: the city plays host to theatrical, dance and music events. Outstanding: INSIDER TIP Flamenco in the Jardines de Sabatini next to the Royal Palace. *veranosdelavilla.com*

FIRST HALF OF AUGUST
Verbena de la Paloma/San Cayetano/San Lorenzo: folk festivals around the Plaza Cascorro in the Rastro barrio and on the Calle Argumosa in Lavapiés.

SEPTEMBER
Dcode Festival: one-day open air-rock festival on the campus of the Universidad Complutense. *dcodefest.com*

LATE OCTOBER–BEGINNING OF JUNE
Festival de Otoño a Primavera: festival with events on many of the city's stages. *www.madrid.org/fo*

NOVEMBER
Madrid en Danza: international dance festival on various city stages. *www.madrid.org/madridendanza*

DECEMBER
Christmas market on the Plaza Mayor
New Year's Eve celebration at the Puerta del Sol – a nationally televised event.

NATIONAL HOLIDAYS

In some years, 19 March *(San José)*, Corpus Christi, 25 July *(Santiago Apóstol)* and 9 Sept *(Santa María de la Cabeza)* are also holidays.

1 Jan	*Año Nuevo*
6 Jan	*Reyes Magos*
March/April	Maundy Thursday *(Jueves Santo)* and Good Friday *(Viernes Santo)*
1 May	*Fiesta del Trabajo*
2 May	*Día de la Comunidad de Madrid*
15 May	*San Isidro*
15 Aug	*Asunción de la Virgen*
12 Oct	*Día de la Hispanidad*
1 Nov	*Todos los Santos*
9 Nov	*Nuestra Señora de la Almudena*
6 Dec	*Día de la Constitución*
8 Dec	*Inmaculada Concepción*
25 Dec	*Navidad*

LINKS, BLOGS, APPS & MORE

www.monumentamadrid.es In pre-digital times you would have needed a lot of shelf space for this collection. Here you'll find photos and text (unfortunately only in Spanish) of practically every building of historical interest

www.centraldereservas.com The Spanish alternative to the international hotel reservations portal, it lists more than 300 hotels in Madrid – also in English

www.deflamenco.com The best flamenco site on the net, also in English

www.30madrid.com The ultimate website for all those visitors who have to count their pennies and where comfort is not everything when it comes to accommodation. Stay the night for under 30 euros per person

www.blogginmadrid.com This extremely useful city blog covers the usual and current topics such as football, attractions and events in Madrid

www.my-little-madrid.com The sisters Almudena and Marcela de la Peña share a passion for their home city and post new tips on how to enjoy Madrid at least once a week on their English language blog

spanishsabores.com Spain travel blog for gourmets and a food blog for travellers who are looking for good places to eat in Madrid

www.facebook.com/RealMadrid Over 80 million fans follow every single game fanatically of this prestigious football club and its stars on its Facebook page

twitter.com/el_pais This is the twitter service by the leading daily newspaper, "El País", that helps you keep abreast of what's happening in Spain and the world

Regardless of whether you are still preparing your trip or already in Madrid: these addresses will provide you with more information, videos and networks to make your holiday even more enjoyable

madrid.angloinfo.com This site is an online network geared to expats living in Madrid and is full of information about the city including the listings for all the English movies showing and an up to date guide on city events

radiocirculo.es local cultural radio show broadcast in several languages from Madrid's Círculo de Bellas Artes

www.youtube.com/watch?v=yQGAsikORI4&feature=related Justo Gallego Martínez has been constructing on his own a cathedral using basic resources in the town of Mejorada del Campo in the Community of Madrid since 1963. It has neither a blueprint or any planning permissions just God's blessing. The story of a mad man or saint

radiocable.com/lacafetera Every morning at half past eight, Fernando Berlín interviews some of Spain's most influential personalities – and has made a name for himself as well

www.youtube.com/watch?v=XQMB5TxdppI Announcement for the 2016 Flamenco Festival – you get a glimpse of some places in the city plus some of its very musical and passionate people

eltenedor Shows you where the best restaurants are located in your area. Reserve a table online (discounts available) at *www.eltenedor.es*

Guia oficial de Madrid useful tourist app from Madrid's tourist information office, English version available, suitable for Android and Apple devices

moovit Not perfect but currently the best app available for the public transport network

VIDEOS & MUSIC

APPS

TRAVEL TIPS

ARRIVAL

Trains from the north arrive at Chamartín station while trains from Barcelona and the south arrive at Atocha station. From here the Metro will get you to your final destination.

Madrid's airport *(www.aena.es)* in the Barajas district only about 15 km/9 miles northeast of the city centre has been named Adolfo Suárez in 2014, after the former Spanish prime minister. The biggest airport in Spain is serviced by a large number of regular direct flights from most major international destinations. Budget airlines like easyJet *(www.easyjet.com)* and Ryanair *(www.ryanair.com)* also have regular connections. For fare comparisons and special deals try websites like *www.farecompare.com, www.expedia.com* and *www.lastminute.com.* After your booking, pay attention to your arrival (and departure) terminal – terminal buildings T1, T2, T3 and T4 are kilometres apart from each other. A taxi to the city centre (within the motorway ring M30) will cost you 30 euros, a fixed price where no surcharges are allowed. Taking the Metro (line 8) is a lot cheaper, either from the Metro station in T4 or the one in T1/T2/T3. It is best to buy a multiple ride ticket (called *metrobus* or *diez viajes)* for 12.20 euros (your travel companions can also use it for their rides). For the journey from or to the airport there is an additional 3 euro airport surcharge *(suplemento aeropuerto)* without which you will not be able to get through the turnstiles at the exit. The journey to the city centre takes about 30–40 minutes. An Airport Express Bus *(www.emtmadrid.es/lineaAeropuerto/index.html)* leaves Terminals 4, 2 and 1 around the clock for the Plaza de a Cibeles and onwards (only between 6am and 11.30pm) for Atocha station. From T4, every half hour line C1 of the fast regional train *(tren de cercanías | www.renfe.com/viajeros/cercanias/madrid)* fleaves for only 2.60 euros to the stations Chamartín, Atocha and Príncipe Pío.

RESPONSIBLE TRAVEL

It doesn't take a lot to be environmentally friendly whilst travelling. Don't just think about your carbon footprint whilst flying to and from your holiday destination but also about how you can protect nature and culture abroad. As a tourist it is especially important to respect nature, look out for local products, cycle instead of driving, save water and much more. If you would like to find out more about eco-tourism please visit: *www.ecotourism.org*

BICYCLES

More than 2000 electric bikes from *BiciMAD,* the public bike rental service *(www.bicimad.com),* are available to hire at over 100 stations spread across the city. Simply use your credit card to purchase a user pass for one, three or five days at any one of the machines next to the rental stations. You'll be charged a deposit of 150 euros which is returned when you pay at the end: the first two hours cost 2 euros and 4 euros for every additional hour.

From arrival to weather

Holiday from start to finish: the most important addresses and information for your Madrid trip

Private bike rental service:
– *Trixi Madrid* (123 D2) *(𝄞 F4)* *(C/ Jardines 12 | www.trixi.com | Metro 1, 2, 3: Sol);* they also offer guided bike tours in English *(March–Nov daily 11am without prebooking)*
– *Bravo Bike* (127 D4) *(𝄞 D3)* *(C/ Juan Álvarez Mendizábal 19 | www.bravobike.com | Metro 3, 10: Plaza de España),* also offering a range of bike tours through Madrid
– *Bike Spain* (122 B3) *(𝄞 E5)* *(Plaza de la Villa 1 | www.bikespain.info | Metro 2, 5: Ópera)*

CONSULATES & EMBASSIES

BRITISH EMBASSY
Tel. +349 17 14 63 00 | ukinspain.fco.gov.uk/en | Paseo de la Castellana 259D | Metro 10: Begoña

U.S. EMBASSY
Tel. +349 15 87 22 00 | madrid.usembassy.gov | Calle Serrano 75 | Metro 5: Rubén Darío

CANADIAN EMBASSY
Tel. +349 13 82 84 00 | www.canadainternational.gc.ca/spain-espagne | Paseo de la Castellana 259D | Metro 10: Begoña

CUSTOMS

UK citizens do not have to pay any duty on goods brought from another EU country as long as tax was included in the price and are for private consumption. The limits are: 800 cigarettes, 400 cigarillo, 200 cigars, 1kg smoking tobacco, 10L spirits, 20L liqueurs, 90L wine, 110L beer. Travellers from the USA, Canada, Australia or other non-EU countries are allowed to enter with the following tax-free amounts: 200 cigarettes or 100 cigarillos or 50 cigars or 250g smoking tobacco. 2L wine and spirits with less 22 vol % alcohol, 1L spirits with more than 22vol % alcohol content.

Travellers to the United States who are returning residents of the country do not have to pay duty on articles purchased overseas up to the value of $800, but there are limits on the amount of alcoholic beverages and tobacco products. For the regulations for international travel for U.S. residents please see *www.cbp.gov*

CURRENCY CONVERTER

£	€	€	£
1	1.17	1	0.85
3	3.50	3	2.56
5	5.86	5	4.26
13	15.24	13	11.09
40	47	40	34.11
75	88	75	63.96
120	141	120	102
250	293	250	213
500	586	500	426

$	€	€	$
1	0.94	1	1.06
3	2.82	3	3.19
5	4.70	5	5.32
13	12.22	13	13.83
40	37.60	40	42.55
75	70.50	75	79.78
120	113	120	128
250	235	250	266
500	470	500	532

For current exchange rates see www.xe.com

EMERGENCY & POLICE

Police, fire, ambulance *tel. 112*
At the police station in *C/ de Leganitos 19* *((122 B1)* *(🏛 E4)* *Metro 2: Santo Domingo)*, the *Servicio de Atención al Turista Extranjero SATE (daily 9am–midnight | tel. 9 15 48 80 08)* takes care of foreign tourists and their emergencies.

EVENTS & TICKET SALES

The city's cultural events are listed in the weekly "Guía del Ocio" *(www.guiadelocio. com/madrid)* or in the Friday supplement of the daily newspaper "El Mundo" *(www. metropoli.com)*. You can make bookings for concerts or the theatre at www.*atrapalo. com*, *www.entradas.com* or *www.ticket master.es* and, of course, on the organiser's website, or ask your hotel for help.

CITY TOURS & SIGHTSEEING TOURS

Madrid City Tour offers a choice of two sightseeing tours through Madrid in an ● open top double-decker bus *(Nov–Feb 10am–6pm approx. every 15 min., March–Oct 9am–10pm approx. every 8 min.)*.Both routes share the same bus stops on the *Fuente Neptuno* *(123 F3)* *(🏛 G5)* next to the Prado, on the *Plaza de la Cibeles* *(123 F2)* *(🏛 G4)*, on the *Plaza de Colón* *(128 C4)* *(🏛 G3)*and on the *Puerta del Sol* *(122–123 C–D 2–3)* *(🏛 F4)*. From mid-June to mid-September there is also a late-night tour at 10pm from the *Fuente de Neptuno* *(123 F3)* *(🏛 G5)* on the Plaza Cánovas del Castillo. The combination ticket for both routes costs 21 euros, for two days 25 euros. You pay on the bus and you can hop on and hop off at any time. There is audio commentary in English. *www.madridcitytour.es*

A number of guided tours and sightseeing tours set out from the *Centro de Turismo de Madrid* *(122 B3)* *(🏛 E5)* *(Plaza Mayor 27 | Metro 1, 2, 3: Sol)* daily. The *Descubre Madrid* takes you on a journey of discovery by foot, bicycle, bus and some of the guides are even dressed in costume. Tours in English and Spanish take you through the secrets and highlights of Madrid's historic old town and through the Retiro. *3.90–7.85 euro | www.esmadrid.com, www.entradas.com*
Segway Trip *(122 B3)* *(🏛 E5)* *(from 25 euros | Plaza de San Miguel 2 | segway trip.com | Metro 2, 5: Ópera)* offers entertaining one-hour tours; a three-hour tour starts at the river, offered by *Madsegs* *(130 C2)* *(🏛 D5)* *(65 euros | Paseo Virgen del Puerto 45 | www.madsegs.com | Metro 6: Puerta del Ángel)*.

HEALTH

If you need a doctor urgently you will need to ask for the closest *hospital* with an emergency room or *urgencia*. Waiting times can be quite long. The Spanish health care system is state-of-the art but tends to be overloaded. If you are a UK or European Union resident your free European Health Insurance Card (EHIC) will allow you access to medical treatment while travelling. If you are treated at a private practise or private clinic you have to pay upfront and then claim from your insurance on your return home. Private medical travel insurance is highly recommended.

IMMIGRATION

Citizens of the UK & Ireland, USA, Canada, Australia and New Zealand need only a valid passport to enter all countries of the EU. Children below the age of 12 need a children's passport.

INFORMATION IN ADVANCE

WEBSITES FOR GENERAL INFORMATION

The following websites are in English:
– *www.spain.info:* official website of the Spanish Tourism Board
– *www.esmadrid.com:* official tourism and event calendar for the city of Madrid
– *www.turismomadrid.es:* website of the Madrid region
– *www.descubremadrid.com:* tourism portal of the Spanish Chamber of Industry and Commerce

INFORMATION IN MADRID

OFICINAS DE TURISMO

City of Madrid: (122 C3) (*M E5*) *Plaza Mayor 27 | tel. 9 14 54 44 10 | Metro 1, 2, 3: Sol | daily. 9.30am–8.30pm*

Comunidad de Madrid (for Madrid and surrounding area): (123 E3) (*M G5*) *C/ Duque de Medinaceli 2 | tel. 9 14 29 49 51 | Metro 2: Banco de España | Mon–Sat 8am–3pm, Sun 9am–2pm*

Additional information kiosks at e.g. Plaza de la Cibeles, Plaza de Callao and Terminals 2 and 4 at Airport Arrivals.

INTERNET ACCESS & WI-FI

The Spaniards also use the word WiFi for wireless Internet. Most hotels and *hostales* now offer their guests free WiFi – simply ask at the reception for the password. It's also normal to ask in cafés and quieter pubs for *"Tiene wi-fi?"* ("Do you have WiFi?"). The lounges of the *Centro Centro* ((123 F2) (*M G4*)

BOOKS & FILMS

The Infatuations – María has become fascinated by the glamorous couple she sees every day in the Madrid cafe where she takes breakfast on her way to work. But then something terrible happens. A masterpiece by Javier Marías about life, love and death.

Death in the Afternoon – This was Ernest Hemingway's second book about bullfighting, first published in 1932 it is a non-fiction account of the customs, traditions and history of bullfighting and matadors. Hemingway was a true fan and famously spent much of his time in Madrid exploring its bars and bullfighting arenas.

The Long March/The Fall of Madrid/Old Friends – Trilogy by Rafael Chirbes giving a riveting account of the social transition of Spain from the Franco dictatorship to a modern European country through the eyes of friends and family in Madrid. A sophisticated masterpiece.

Goya's Ghosts – A film that covers the life of the exceptional artist Francisco de Goya during the turmoil at the end of the 18th century at the time of the Spanish Inquisition and the French Revolution. The Retiro is one of the many backdrops. Directed by Milos Forman (2006).

Abre los ojos – Titled "Open your Eyes" (1997) for English audiences, this is a film by Alejandro Amenábar (Spain's most successful director after film doyen Pedro Almodóvar) is a mystery drama that has some unusual shots of Madrid e.g. the unusually deserted Gran Vía.

BUDGETING

Coffee	around £1.30/$1.60 *for a café solo*
Snack	from £1.50/$1.90 *for a small tapa*
Wine	around £2.50/$3.20 *for a glass*
Clubbing	around £13/$16 *entrance fee at the weekend*
Metro	£1.30/$1.60 *for a single journey*
Museum	£12/$15 *entrance fee at the Prado*

Metro 2: Banco de España) in the Palacio de Cibeles on the Plaza de Cibeles or in *Mercado San Antón* ((123 E1) *(M G3)* C/ Augusto Figueroa

24 | *Metro 5: Chueca)* in Chueca also offer use of the Internet.

MADRID CARD

You can get a card from any of the *oficinas de turismo,* travel agencies or on the Internet. It allows you free admission to almost all of Madrid's museums and to a Bernabéu stadium tour. Cardholders also avoid the long queues at the Prado or Thyssen-Bornemisza museums and other perks are a tour of the city and discounts at select restaurants, shops or flamenco *tablaos.* The card costs 47 euros for one day, 60 euros for two, 67 euros for three and 77 euros for five days (six to twelve year olds 32/42/44/47 euros). www.madridcard.com

MONEY & CREDIT CARDS

You will find banks with ATMs *(cajero automático)* on every corner. Most hotels

WEATHER IN MADRID

	Jan	Feb	March	April	May	June	July	Aug	Sept	Oct	Nov	Dec
Daytime temperatures in °C/°F	8/46	11/52	14/57	18/64	22/72	27/81	31/88	30/86	25/77	19/66	12/54	9/48
Nighttime temperatures in °C/°F	1/34	2/36	4/39	7/45	10/50	14/57	17/63	17/63	13/55	9/48	4/39	2/36
Sunshine hours/day	5	6	6	8	9	11	13	11	9	6	5	5
Precipitation days/month	7	7	8	7	6	4	2	1	4	6	8	7

and restaurants, as well as many shops, accept credit cards – the most common are Visa and MasterCard.

PARKING

If you are planning to visit Madrid by car, be sure to book your garage parking in advance with your hotel. Parking bays painted with green lines are for residents only, visitors use those marked blue.

PHONE & MOBILE PHONE

Dialling codes from Spain: UK *+44*, United States *+1* and to dial Spain from abroad *+34* (remember to drop the first *0* of the city code). When making a domestic call in Spain you need to dial the entire nine digit number. Spanish mobile phone numbers begin with *6* or, more seldom, a *7*. Roaming is not that expensive anymore.

POST

Post office *(oficinas de correos)* opening times generally: *Mon–Fri 8.30am–2.30pm, Sat 9.30am–1pm.* It can be quicker to buy stamps in the *estanco* (tobacco shop or news stand). Postage abroad to the rest of Europe is 90 cents. *www.correos.es*

PUBLIC TRANSPORT

The Metro *(www.metromadrid.es)* is the best means of transportation in Madrid. It has 15 underground lines (an overview map can be found on the inside back cover) and is operational from 6am to 1.30am. The trains run every three to five minutes in the rush hour but late at night the intervals can be up to 15 minutes. You can catch a night bus at the Plaza de la Cibeles between midnight and 6am. There are 26 bus routes to the suburbs.

A single ticket costs 1.50 euro, a multiple ride ticket *(metrobus* or *diez viajes)* 12.20 euros and there are ticket vending machines at the entrance to all the stations. You can change trains as often as you want to during one journey. The multiple ride ticket can also be used on the red buses of Madrid's EMT *(www.emtmadrid. es).* With the bus service you have to validate your ticket every time you change buses. There is also the *Abono turístico*, a ticket valid for one, two, three, five or seven days (8.40–35.40 euros, children aged 4–10 years pay half price). Generally Zone A is all you'll need. Zone T (17–70.80 euros) is only worth it if you intend to explore the surrounding countryside as well.

The *trenes de cercanía* run by the Renfe *(www.renfe.es)* railway company is a rapid urban rail service that also services the suburbs. Their stations are signposted with a white C in italics against a red background. The metrobus ticket is not valid for the *cercanías*.

TAXI

If you need a taxi just wave from the curb. A green light on the roof indicates that the taxi is available. The meter starts at 2.40 euros. Journeys to and from the airport have a fixed price of 30 euros while journeys from train stations incur a 3 euro surcharge. A taxi ride will cost more between 9pm and 7am as well as on weekends. To call a taxi dial *9 15 47 82 00.*

TIPS

Only tip what you deem appropriate. In restaurants five to ten per cent is the norm. In a taxi you simply round off the figure. Tip a porter or chambermaid 1 euro.

USEFUL PHRASES SPANISH

PRONUNCIATION

c	before "e" and "i" like "th" in "thin"
ch	as in English
g	before "e" and "i" like the "ch" in Scottish "loch"
gue, gui	like "get", "give"
que, qui	the "u" is not spoken, i.e. "ke", "ki"
j	always like the "ch" in Scottish "loch"
ll	like "lli" in "million"; some speak it like "y" in "yet"
ñ	"nj"
z	like "th" in "thin"

IN BRIEF

Yes/No/Maybe	sí/no/quizás
Please/Thank you	por favor/gracias
Hello!/Goodbye!/See you	¡Hola!/¡Adiós!/¡Hasta luego!
Good morning!/afternoon!/evening!/night!	¡Buenos días!/¡Buenos días!/¡Buenas tardes!/¡Buenas noches!
Excuse me, please!	¡Perdona!/¡Perdone!
May I...?/Pardon?	¿Puedo...?/¿Cómo dice?
My name is ...	Me llamo...
What's your name?	¿Cómo se llama usted?/¿Cómo te llamas?
I'm from ...	Soy de...
I would like to .../Have you got ...?	Querría.../¿Tiene usted...?
How much is ...?	¿Cuánto cuesta...?
I (don't) like that	Esto (no) me gusta.
good/bad/broken/doesn't work	bien/mal/roto/no funciona
too much/much/little/all/nothing	demasiado/mucho/poco/todo/nada
Help!/Attention!/Caution!	¡Socorro!/¡Atención!/¡Cuidado!
ambulance/police/fire brigade	ambulancia/policía/bomberos
May I take a photo here	¿Podría fotografiar aquí?

DATE & TIME

Monday/Tuesday/Wednesday	lunes/martes/miércoles
Thursday/Friday/Saturday	jueves/viernes/sábado
Sunday/working day/holiday	domingo/laborable/festivo
today/tomorrow/yesterday	hoy/mañana/ayer

¿Hablas español?

"Do you speak Spanish?" This guide will help you to say the basic words and phrases in Spanish

hour/minute/second/moment	hora/minuto/segundo/momento
day/night/week/month/year	día/noche/semana/mes/año
now/immediately/before/after	ahora/enseguida/antes/después
What time is it?	¿Qué hora es?
It's three o'clock/It's half past three	Son las tres/Son las tres y media
a quarter to four/a quarter past four	cuatro menos cuarto/ cuatro y cuarto

TRAVEL

open/closed/opening times	abierto/cerrado/horario
entrance / exit	entrada/acceso salida
departure/arrival	salida/llegada
toilets/ladies/gentlemen	aseos/señoras/caballeros
free/occupied	libre/ocupado
(not) drinking water	agua (no) potable
Where is ...?/Where are ...?	¿Dónde está...? /¿Dónde están ...?
left/right	izquierda/derecha
straight ahead/back	recto/atrás
close/far	cerca/lejos
traffic lights/corner/crossing	semáforo/esquina/cruce
bus/tram/U-underground/	autobús/tranvía/metro/
taxi/cab	taxi
bus stop/cab stand	parada/parada de taxis
parking lot/parking garage	parking/garaje
street map/map	plano de la ciudad/mapa
train station/harbour/airport	estación/puerto/aeropuerto
ferry/quay	transbordador/muelle
schedule/ticket/supplement	horario/billete/suplemento
single/return	sencillo/ida y vuelta
train/track/platform	tren/vía/andén
delay/strike	retraso/huelga
I would like to rent ...	Querría... alquilar
a car/a bicycle/a boat	un coche/una bicicleta/un barco
petrol/gas station	gasolinera
petrol/gas / diesel	gasolina/diesel
breakdown/repair shop	avería/taller

FOOD & DRINK

Could you please book a table for tonight for four?	Resérvenos, por favor, una mesa para cuatro personas para hoy por la noche.
on the terrace/by the window	en la terraza/junto a la ventana

The menu, please/	¡El menú, por favor!
Could I please have ...?	¿Podría traerme... por favor?
bottle/carafe/glass	botella/jarra/vaso
knife/fork/spoon	cuchillo/tenedor/cuchara
salt/pepper/sugar	sal/pimienta/azúcar
vinegar/oil/milk/cream/lemon	vinagre/aceite/leche/limón
cold/too salty/not cooked	frío/demasiado salado/sin hacer
with/without ice/sparkling	con/sin hielo/gas
vegetarian/allergy	vegetariano/vegetariana/alergía
May I have the bill, please?	Querría pagar, por favor.
bill/receipt/tip	cuenta/recibo/propina

SHOPPING

pharmacy/chemist	farmacia/droguería
baker/market	panadería/mercado
butcher/fishmonger	carnicería/pescadería
shopping centre/department store	centro comercial/grandes almacenes
shop/supermarket/kiosk	tienda/supermercado/quiosco
100 grammes/1 kilo	cien gramos/un kilo
expensive/cheap/price/more/less	caro/barato/precio/más/menos
organically grown	de cultivo ecológico

ACCOMMODATION

I have booked a room	He reservado una habitación.
Do you have any ... left?	¿Tiene todavía...?
single room/double room	habitación individual/habitación doble
breakfast/half board/	desayuno/media pensión/
full board (American plan)	pensión completa
at the front/seafront/garden view	hacia delante/hacia el mar/hacia el jardín
shower/sit-down bath	ducha/baño
balcony/terrace	balcón/terraza
key/room card	llave/tarjeta
luggage/suitcase/bag	equipaje/maleta/bolso
swimming pool/spa/sauna	piscina/spa/sauna
soap/toilet paper/nappy (diaper)	jabón/papel higiénico/pañal
cot/high chair/nappy changing	cuna/trona/cambiar los pañales
deposit	anticipo/caución

BANKS, MONEY & CREDIT CARDS

bank/ATM/	banco/cajero automático/
pin code	número secreto
cash/credit card	en efectivo/tarjeta de crédito
bill/coin/change	billete/moneda/cambio

HEALTH

doctor/dentist/paediatrician	médico/dentista/pediatra
hospital/emergency clinic	hospital/urgencias
fever/pain/inflamed/injured	fiebre/dolor/inflamado/herido
diarrhoea/nausea/sunburn	diarrea/náusea/quemadura de sol
plaster/bandage/ointment/cream	tirita/vendaje/pomada/crema
pain reliever/tablet/suppository	calmante/comprimido/supositorio

POST, TELECOMMUNICATIONS & MEDIA

stamp/letter/postcard	sello/carta/postal
I need a landline phone card/	Necesito una tarjeta telefónica/
I'm looking for a prepaid card for my mobile	Busco una tarjeta prepago para mi móvil
Where can I find internet access?	¿Dónde encuentro un acceso a internet?
dial/connection/engaged	marcar/conexión/ocupado
socket/adapter/charger	enchufe/adaptador/cargador
computer/battery/	ordenador/batería/
rechargeable battery	batería recargable
e-mail address/at sign (@)	(dirección de) correo electrónico/arroba
internet address (URL)	dirección de internet
internet connection/wifi	conexión a internet/wifi
e-mail/file/print	archivo/imprimir

LEISURE, SPORTS & BEACH

beach/sunshade/lounger	playa/sombrilla/tumbona
low tide/high tide/current	marea baja/marea alta/corriente

NUMBERS

0	cero	14	catorce
1	un, uno, una	15	quince
2	dos	16	dieciséis
3	tres	17	diecisiete
4	cuatro	18	dieciocho
5	cinco	19	diecinueve
6	seis	20	veinte
7	siete	100	cien, ciento
8	ocho	200	doscientos, doscientas
9	nueve	1000	mil
10	diez	2000	dos mil
11	once	10 000	diez mil
12	doce	1/2	medio
13	trece	1/4	un cuarto

STREET ATLAS

The green line indicates the Discovery Tour "Madrid at a glance"
The blue line indicates the other Discovery Tours

All tours are also marked on the pull-out map

Photo: Plaza de Oriente in front of the Palacio Real

Exploring Madrid

The map on the back cover shows how the area has been sub-divided

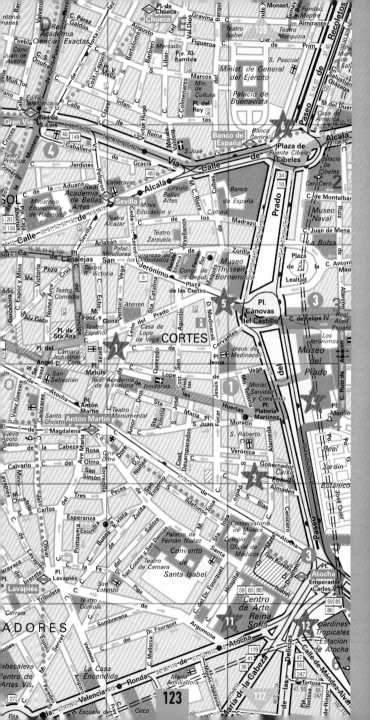

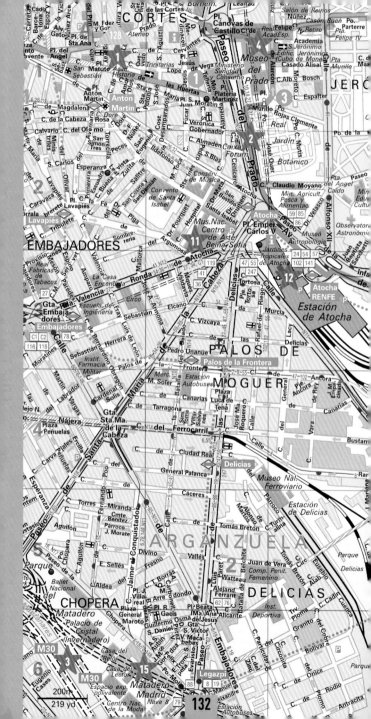

Trav. Suspiro del Moro
Trv.Quijada de Pandiellos
C.Monte Naranco

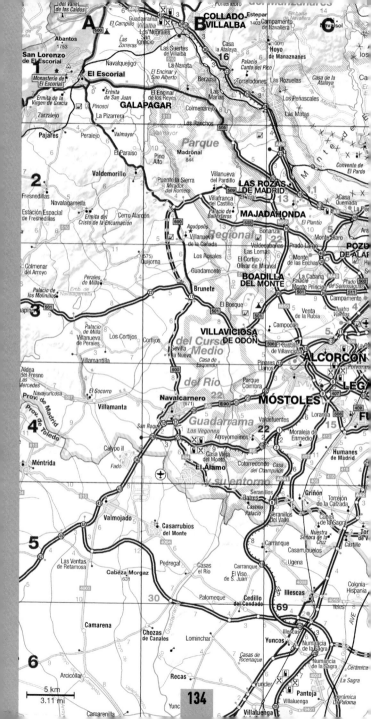

135

This index lists a selection of the streets and squares shown in the street atlas

KEY TO STREET ATLAS

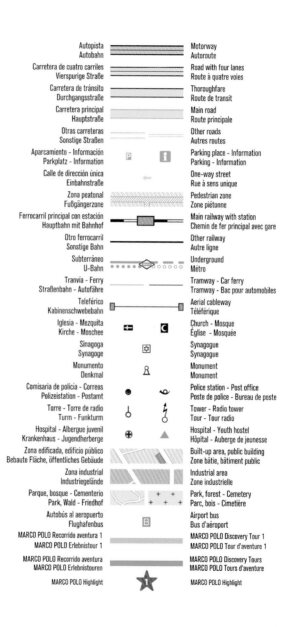

Autopista / Autobahn	Motorway / Autoroute
Carretera de cuatro carriles / Vierspurige Straße	Road with four lanes / Route à quatre voies
Carretera de tránsito / Durchgangsstraße	Thoroughfare / Route de transit
Carretera principal / Hauptstraße	Main road / Route principale
Otras carreteras / Sonstige Straßen	Other roads / Autres routes
Aparcamiento - Información / Parkplatz - Information	Parking place - Information / Parking - Information
Calle de dirección única / Einbahnstraße	One-way street / Rue à sens unique
Zona peatonal / Fußgängerzone	Pedestrian zone / Zone piétonne
Ferrocarril principal con estación / Hauptbahn mit Bahnhof	Main railway with station / Chemin de fer principal avec gare
Otro ferrocarril / Sonstige Bahn	Other railway / Autre ligne
Subterráneo / U-Bahn	Underground / Métro
Tranvía - Ferry / Straßenbahn - Autofähre	Tramway - Car ferry / Tramway - Bac pour automobiles
Teleférico / Kabinenschwebebahn	Aerial cableway / Téléférique
Iglesia - Mezquita / Kirche - Moschee	Church - Mosque / Église - Mosquée
Sinagoga / Synagoge	Synagogue / Synagogue
Monumento / Denkmal	Monument / Monument
Comisaría de policía - Correos / Polizeistation - Postamt	Police station - Post office / Poste de police - Bureau de poste
Torre - Torre de radio / Turm - Funkturm	Tower - Radio tower / Tour - Tour radio
Hospital - Albergue juvenil / Krankenhaus - Jugendherberge	Hospital - Youth hostel / Hôpital - Auberge de jeunesse
Zona edificada, edificio público / Bebaute Fläche, öffentliches Gebäude	Built-up area, public building / Zone bâtie, bâtiment public
Zona industrial / Industriegelände	Industrial area / Zone industrielle
Parque, bosque - Cementerio / Park, Wald - Friedhof	Park, forest - Cemetery / Parc, bois - Cimetière
Autobús al aeropuerto / Flughafenbus	Airport bus / Bus d'aéroport
MARCO POLO Recorrido aventura 1 / MARCO POLO Erlebnistour 1	MARCO POLO Discovery Tour 1 / MARCO POLO Tour d'aventure 1
MARCO POLO Recorrido aventura / MARCO POLO Erlebnistouren	MARCO POLO Discovery Tours / MARCO POLO Tours d'aventure
MARCO POLO Highlight	MARCO POLO Highlight

MARCO POLO TRAVEL GUIDES

The travel guides with
**Insider
Tips**

INDEX

This index lists all sights and museums featured in this guide.
Numbers in bold indicate a main entry

CREDITS

WRITE TO US

e-mail: info@marcopologuides.co.uk

Did you have a great holiday? Is there something on your mind? Whatever it is, let us know! Whether you want to praise, alert us to errors or give us a personal tip – MARCO POLO would be pleased to hear from you. We do everything we can to provide the very latest information for your trip.

Nevertheless, despite all of our authors' thorough research, errors can creep in. MARCO POLO does not accept any liability for this. Please contact us by e-mail or post.

MARCO POLO Travel Publishing Ltd
Pinewood, Chineham Business Park
Crockford Lane, Chineham
Basingstoke, Hampshire RG24 8AL
United Kingdom

PICTURE CREDITS
Cover photograph: Gran Vía (Laif: Knechtel)
Photos: DuMont Bildarchiv: Huber (30); R. Freyer (6, 104, 104/105, 106/107); Getty Images: R. M. Gill (62 l.); huber-images: P. Giocoso (flap top, 20/21, 52/53, 92/93), S. Kremer (7, 26/27, 33), A. Pavan (8), S. Raccanello (11, 19 top, 120/121), M. Ripani (51); R. Irek (44/45); La Casita De Wendy (18 centre); Laif: Celentano (4 top), Huber (107), Knechtel: 1; Raach (54), Westrich (10); Laif/REA: Fourmy (68); Look: Pompe (66/67); Look/age fotostock (87); mauritius images: C. Seba (82/83), J. Ulmer (25); mauritius images/age (40, 109); mauritius images/Alamy (flap bottom, 2/3, 9, 12/13, 17, 18 top, 18 bottom, 19 bottom, 46/47, 55, 58, 61, 62 right, 64, 84/85, 86, 89, 90, 98/99, 103, 105, 108 bottom); mauritius images/CuboImags (37); mauritius images/Imagebroker: S. Kiefer (22, 42, 49); mauritius images/imagebroker: von Poser (5, 76); mauritius images/Imagebroker: M. Weber (34); mauritius images/Imagebroker/White Star: A. Mateo (108 top); mauritius images/Quickimage (70/71); T. Stankiewicz (14/15, 72); White Star: M. Gumm (4 bottom, 41, 56/57, 74/75, 78), Steinert (38, 106)

2nd Edition – fully revised and updated 2017
Worldwide Distribution: Marco Polo Travel Publishing Ltd, Pinewood, Chineham Business Park, Crockford Lane, Basingstoke, Hampshire RG24 8AL, United Kingdom. Email: sales@marcopolouk.com
© MAIRDUMONT GmbH & Co. KG, Ostfildern
Chief editor: Marion Zorn
Author: Martin Dahms; editor: Nikolai Michaelis
Programme supervision: Susanne Heimburger, Tamara Hub, Nikolai Michaelis, Kristin Schimpf, Martin Silbermann
Picture editor: Gabriele Forst; What's hot: wunder media, Munich
Cartography street atlas & pull-out map: © MAIRDUMONT, Ostfildern
Design: milchhof: atelier, Berlin; Front cover, pull-out map cover, page 1: factor product munich; Discovery Tours: Susan Chaaban, Dipl.-Des. (FH)
Translated from German by Birgitt Lederer; Susan Jones; editor of the English edition: Margaret Howie, fullproof.co.za
Prepress: writehouse, Cologne; InterMedia, Ratingen
Phrase book in cooperation with Ernst Klett Sprachen GmbH, Stuttgart, Editorial by Pons Wörterbücher

DOS & DON'TS ☞

A few things you should bear in mind in Madrid

DON'T CLAP ALONG

Especially not when the flamenco is being played. The artistic *palmas* form part of the music. There may be the occasional person in the audience who has the right feel for the rhythm – but a newly arrived tourist is not likely to.

DO AS THE LOCALS

A kiss on the left cheek then one on the right is how the Spanish greet one another, just as people would shake hands elsewhere in the world, so don't read anything more into it!

DON'T LIGHT UP

Strict anti-tobacco laws are in force in Spain. Smoking is prohibited in all public buildings, as well as cafés, restaurants, bars and clubs. Even designated smoking areas have been abolished so if you want to smoke you have to go outside.

DO TAKE THE RIGHT TAXI

When you arrive at the airport in Barajas you will see queues of passengers patiently waiting for taxis. Some taxi drivers scout the arrivals for their prey: newly arrived tourists. They will take you straight to their vehicle only to charge you astronomical prices once you arrive at your destination. So it's best to wait your turn at the taxi departure point like everyone else.

DO AVOID PIRATED GOODS

Everywhere in the city centre you'll come across young men – mostly Africans – selling hundreds of pirated CDs and DVDs which they spread out on a blanket before them. The CDs sell for 3 euro, DVDs for 6 euro. Not only is it illegal to buy from these vendors but you are also doing them no favours – they usually earn very little while the ringleaders make the money.

DO TAKE CARE AT TRAFFIC LIGHTS

Madrileños tend to use traffic lights only as a guideline. While you stick to the rules, you can't be sure other cars will. The locals also have a scary habit of going through traffic lights late on orange. Do keep your wits about you and your eyes peeled.

DO LEAVE YOUR VALUABLES BEHIND

Carry as few valuable as possible on you. Be vigilant on the Metro and in crowded places, especially if everyone is pushing and shoving. Be wary of two or three people trying to talk to you at the same time and of people who claim to be plain clothes police.